The Ch[...]

A DOG WALKER'S GUIDE

Ruth Paley

COUNTRYSIDE BOOKS
NEWBURY BERKSHIRE

Countryside Books
3 Catherine Road
Newbury
Berkshire
RG14 7NA

To view our complete range of books please visit us at
www.countrysidebooks.co.uk

First published 2015
·Text © 2015 Ruth Paley
Photographs © 2015 Ruth Paley

Cover photograph © C Howe, Chiltern Society PhotoGroup
A view north over Barton village, west to Sharpenhoe Clappers,
and east over Hitchin to the hills near Royston.

A CIP record for this book is available from the British Library.

ISBN 978 1 84674 331 3

Produced by The Letterworks Ltd., Reading
Typeset by KT Designs, St Helens
Printed by Berforts Information Press, Oxford

Contents

Walk

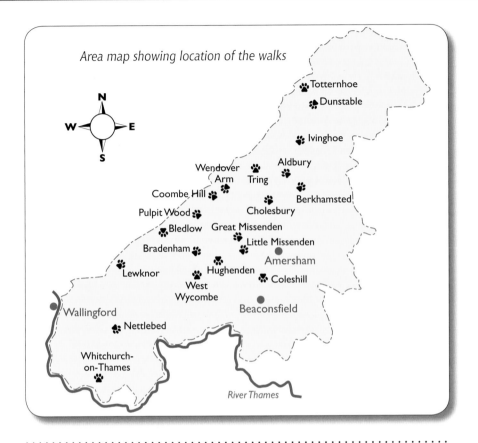

Area map showing location of the walls

Totternhoe
Dunstable

Ivinghoe

Wendover
Arm   Tring   Aldbury

Coombe Hill

Pulpit Wood   Cholesbury   Berkhamsted

Bledlow   Great Missenden

Bradenham   Little Missenden

Lewknor   Hughenden   Amersham

West   Coleshill
Wycombe

Wallingford   Beaconsfield

Nettlebed

Whitchurch-
on-Thames

River Thames

. . . .

PUBLISHER'S NOTE

We hope that you obtain considerable enjoyment from this book; great care has been taken in its preparation. Although at the time of publication all routes followed public rights of way or permitted paths, diversion orders can be made and permissions withdrawn.

We cannot, of course, be held responsible for such diversion orders and any inaccuracies in the text which result from these or any other changes to the routes nor any damage which might result from walkers trespassing on private property. We are anxious though that all details covering the walks are kept up to date and would therefore welcome information from readers which would be relevant to future editions.

The simple sketch maps that accompany the walks in this book are based on notes made by the author whilst checking out the routes on the ground. They are designed to show you how to reach the start, to point out the main features of the overall circuit and they contain a progression of numbers that relate to the paragraphs of the text.

However, for the benefit of a proper map, we do recommend that you purchase the relevant Ordnance Survey sheet covering your walk. The Ordnance Survey maps are widely available, especially through booksellers and local newsagents.

INTRODUCTION

This book aims to take the worry out of walking somewhere new with your dog. These 20 circular dog walks have all been tried and tested, by 2 and 4 legs, to make sure they work for both people and their dogs. There is plenty of safe off-lead time for sniffing and exploring, while avoiding busy roads and stiles. I have a whippet and I know that walking through a field of sheep with a dog pulling on the lead is not relaxing. You can't always avoid livestock, but I have warned you in advance of when you need your dog on a lead, and when you can relax and leave him free to roam. And for the owners I've picked routes in the most beautiful parts of the wonderful Chilterns.

The rolling landscape of the Chilterns is perfect walking country, with its beech-fringed hills and valleys, canals and woods. Many of these circuits take you through carefully managed National Trust land, for example, in the Hughenden, Ashridge and Bradenham Estates, Coombe Hill, Pulpit Wood and West Wycombe. There are also plenty of opportunities to follow the ancient Ridgeway as it winds its way across the Chiltern Hills to the top of Ivinghoe Beacon. I've deliberately started the majority of the walks in villages. This not only helps with navigation and parking, but the villages are well worth exploring at the end of a walk. On these walks I've discovered friendly pubs with dog bowls and large beer gardens, ponds, commons, windmills and even a large pottery kiln at Nettlebed.

You can't walk in the Chilterns without spotting the iconic red kite swooping in the skies above you. You also can't walk without coming across some of the friendliest dog walkers it has been my pleasure to meet. While pausing to study my OS map in woods and fields I have chatted with the helpful owners of many dogs, large and small, who have stopped to offer advice and pass the time of day.

Of course dogs need walking all year round, and with the right shoes you can do all of these walks at any time of the year. But on a hot summer's day with a clear blue sky there is no finer place than the top of Coombe Hill, Ivinghoe Beacon or the Dunstable Downs, with a gentle breeze and a magnificent view. In spring, the beech woods are awash with bluebells, while on misty autumn afternoons, strolling past trees cloaked in yellow and orange leaves is a joy. For crisp winter days the walks by the reservoirs near Tring or by the canal at Berkhamsted offer a firmer path underfoot. Whatever the weather, you will find plenty of walks to suit you and your hound, and you will soon discover why I love walking with my whippet in the Chilterns.

Acknowledgements

To my dad, Chips and Albie for always being enthusiastic 2 and 4 legged walking companions.

Ruth Paley

ADVICE FOR DOG WALKERS

● All dog owners should be aware of the **Countryside Code** regarding dogs: 'By law, you must keep your dog under effective control so that it does not disturb or scare farm animals or wildlife. On most areas of open country and common land, known as 'access land' you must keep your dog on a short lead between 1 March and 31 July, and all year round near farm animals.'

● Do not let your dog disturb **ground-nesting birds**. Unhatched and young birds will soon die without protection from their parents, and your dog running near the nest might be enough to scare the adult birds away. The nesting period is 1 March to 31 July. Keep your dog in sight and near the path, and don't let him roam into the middle of fields where birds such as skylarks might be nesting.

● Bring **water and a bowl**. I noticed that the majority of these walks don't pass anywhere where your dog can stop for a drink, so make sure he doesn't go thirsty.

● These walks all pass through **farmland** and the Chiltern Hills are the ideal terrain for grazing **sheep**. I have indicated where I found sheep, but fields change their use so keep an ear out as you walk. You can normally hear sheep before you see them. Also check each field before letting your dog loose to make sure there are no livestock. If there are sheep you must always have your dog on a lead. The worry of a dog can cause a sheep to miscarry. Under the Dogs (Protection of Livestock) Act there is a fine of up to £1,000 for worrying livestock, which includes not having your dog on a lead in a field of sheep, even if he doesn't harm them.

● In a field of **cattle**, the advice is different. Keep your dog on a lead and give the cows a wide berth. Be particularly careful if they have calves and if possible avoid walking through the field. But if you find yourself surrounded by a herd of curious cattle, drop the lead and get out of the field. Your dog will be able to escape faster without you. I haven't come across many cattle while walking for this book, and the odd time I did the field was large and the animals were easy to avoid. Please also follow any farmers' signs asking for dogs to be kept on a lead.

● **Pick up after your dog**, I have said where there are dog bins. Please don't leave plastic dog bags lying around. They won't disappear and are dangerous to wildlife. If you are far from a dog bin, pick up a stick and flick it into the hedge where it will decompose and not be trodden on.

● It is a good idea to check your dog for **ticks** after a walk, especially if he has been in a wooded area or in bracken. If you find a tick, you have to remove it as soon as possible. Use tweezers, or better still get a special tick remover from a pet shop. Grasp the tick as close as possible to the skin. Then pull the tick straight out without squeezing or twisting it. You can apply products to your dog to prevent ticks and fleas. There are contact details for the nearest vets in the Dog factors box for each walk.

● Finally **look after yourself** by wearing decent walking shoes as the Chiltern Hills go up as well as down and grassy paths can get slippery. Also keep a compass or fully charged smart phone with you to keep an eye on which direction you are walking in, as well as an OS map. I have made the directions as clear as possible, but it is easy to get disorientated in the middle of a wood and there are lots of lovely woods in this book. If in doubt, ask a passing dog walker. They are normally locals and the Chiltern dog walkers are invariably a very friendly and helpful bunch!

Following the Thames Path at Whitchurch

The 18th-century Basildon Park glimpsed across the river Thames.

Where the Chiltern Hills dip down to meet the Thames nestles the pretty village of Whitchurch-on-Thames. This walk follows the Thames Path as it winds through beech woods, with stunning views across the river towards the National Trust's Basildon Park. The views are why you will remember this energetic walk, as the path falls and rises through woodland and past lush meadows. The majority of the walk is safe off-lead time, with the odd chance for a thirsty dog to scramble down to the river for a quick drink and dip in the water. You will also feel close to the red kites as you walk through this peaceful high ground with no sound except the cry of the kites, and the wind in the beech trees.

Terrain
This is an energetic walk with uphill and downhill sections. The fields in the middle section can get muddy.

Where to park
Find a roadside spot either on the High Street in Whitchurch, or on Manor Road, which is off the High Street. (GR 635773) **OS map:** Explorer 171 Chiltern Hills West, or 159 Reading.

How to get there
Whitchurch is on the river Thames opposite Pangbourne. The river is spanned by an iconic toll bridge with a 40p charge to cross each way (which may soon rise to 60p) so if you are travelling from the south have some spare change to hand. From the M4, come off at junction 12 and follow the A4 signed to Theale and Reading. At the next roundabout take the third exit for the A340. In Pangbourne follow the High Street then take the first exit on the second roundabout to cross the Thames to Whitchurch.

Refreshments
There are two dog-friendly pubs in Whitchurch-on-Thames, both are full of character, serve food and have beer gardens. The Ferryboat Inn ☎ 0118 984 2161 is by the bridge and the Greyhound ☎ 0118 984 4800 is further up the High Street.

Dog factors
Distance: 5½ miles
Road walking: Along the pavement at the start of the walk for about 100 yards and about 200 yards at the end (the first part of this section has no pavement).
Livestock: Cattle at point 5 and horses at point 6
Stiles: None
Nearest vets: Shinfield Road Veterinary Surgery, Alstonby, Shinfield Road, Reading RG2 9BE ☎ 0118 987 2294, or Oakley Veterinary Clinic, 65 Oakley Road, Caversham RG4 7RN ☎ 0118 947 9298

The Walk

1 Walk up the **High Street** heading out of the village with the river behind you. Just before the 40 mph signs, turn left to follow the **Thames Path** (the sign for the footpath is on the other side of the road). The tarmac drive leads you past a wooden fence, then continue straight ahead along a more unsurfaced path. Almost immediately you are rewarded with wonderful views across green meadows edged with beech trees. Your dog is safe off lead now as the path is fenced off from the fields.

2 When the path divides at the entrance to **Hartslock Farm**, take the right fork leading steeply down, still with that amazing view on your right. Although the path here is steep, there are steps so you don't have to worry about slipping. Once at the bottom of the dip, the path leads back uphill with hedgerows then meadows either side. As you head through Hartslock Wood the Thames Path once more follows the banks of the river with a dramatic drop on the left down to the water. My dog couldn't resist scrambling down the slope for a drink. Look through the trees and you can catch the odd glimpse of Basildon Park on the opposite bank. Look out for the occasional blue arrow

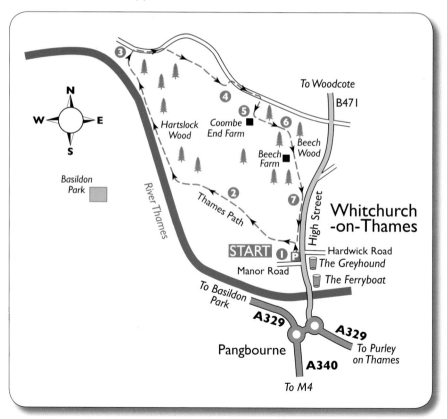

Albie enjoying some off-lead time in the woods.

footpath sign to show you the way. You pass a Second World War pillbox built to defend the Thames against a German invasion. The Thames Path turns to the left along this track, but for this walk continue ahead until you come to a crossing by **Gattendon Lodge**.

3 Turn right and walk, with Gattendon Lodge on your right, up a lane and turn right on to a surfaced lane. Now walk with a hill on your left and the Thames on your right. When this lane veers to the left, turn right onto a shady path under trees. Follow this path uphill with a wonderful view on your right.

4 When you come to a footpath on your left, follow it for a few yards until you come to a cross track where you turn right on a surfaced path. Eventually you come to two cottages on your right numbered 6 and 5. Walk ahead for another 200 yards, then turn right following a sign for **Chiltern Way Extension**. There is an old harrow by the start of this path and a sign for Coombe End Farm.

5 You are heading towards farmland now where there are cattle so put your dog back on a lead. Pass a house on the left, and when the drive branches, go left. Walk ahead for about 80 yards to a kissing gate opposite the barns of **Coombe End Farm**. Walk across a series of fields divided by kissing gates. You can spot the gate on the other side of the field each time. These fields have cattle grazing so dogs on a lead. This is the muddy part of the walk, particularly around the gates.

6 The last kissing gate leads you into the appropriately named **Beech Wood**, where you walk straight ahead, with a fence on your left. Leave the wood through a kissing gate and turn right to walk by a fence across the edge of a paddock, then out of the field by the side of **Beech Farm**. Cross the drive and follow the footpath sign to the right, across a patch of grass then through a kissing gate. Keep going in the same direction along a footpath with brambles either side. You finally come to a large field with electricity wires heading across it. Walk ahead in the same direction as the wires, following the edge of the field then head down a short path to the Whitchurch road.

7 Turn right and walk back down to the village. There is no footpath initially, but soon you will recognise the start of the walk and can stroll along the pavement back to your car, admiring the cottages as you go.

Nettlebed and the Chilterns Way

The dog-friendly White Hart in Nettlebed.

This walk gives your hound plenty of opportunities to stretch his legs and explore some fine Chiltern beech woods. The route starts in an historic village with a restored brick pot kiln and a country inn. The White Hart is a very comfortable and welcoming pub that dates back to the 14th century. There is a pretty garden to sit in, and dogs are welcome inside. The walk follows the Chilterns Way along a country lane to explore flower-rich meadows then the peaceful tranquility of beech woodland carpeted with bluebells and wood anemones in spring, by the Warburg Nature Reserve. We met very few people on this walk and I would recommend it as an ideal stroll if you want to relax at the end of a busy week in some classic Chilterns countryside.

The Chilterns – A Dog Walker's Guide

Terrain

A mostly level route along field paths and woods. There are some slight uphill sections in the woods, and under the shade of the trees it could get muddy in the winter or after rain.

Where to park

You can park at the White Hart if you are eating there, otherwise find a spot by the village common (GR 702868). **OS map:** Explorer 171 Chiltern Hills West.

How to get there

Nettlebed is on the A4130, halfway between Henley-on-Thames and Wallingford. As you drive through the village, the common and pub are both easy to spot.

Refreshments

The White Hart in Nettlebed has an impressive website and menu, and welcomes dogs, both on the veranda where there are large tables with parasols for a sunny day, or in the pub. It is only in the restaurant area that dogs cannot go. There is a bowl of water outside for thirsty hounds. ☎ 01491 641245.

Dog factors
. . . .

Distance: 3 miles
Road walking: A little at the start and end of the walk in Nettlebed, but there is a pavement.
Livestock: There may be cows in the field at point 3.
Stiles: None
Nearest vets: Shinfield Road Veterinary Surgery, Alstonby, Shinfield Road, Reading RG2 9BE ☎ 0118 987 2294

The Walk
. . . .

1 From the White Hart, turn left and walk along the **High Street**. Cross **Watlington Street** to the village shelter (don't go as far as the bus shelter). As you pass it is worth stopping to have a look at the pot kiln and its information board. *There would once have been several of these bottle-shaped brick kilns in the village, but the others have all been removed so this is the only preserved bottle kiln in the county. The brick, tile and pot industry existed in Nettlebed from* *the Middle Ages until the early 20th century. Clay for the bricks was dug up from Nettlebed Common, the bricks were baked in the kiln and many of the houses you see in the village were built with these bricks.* Follow the lane between the common and the cottages, with the village shelter on your right. Stay on the lane under the trees to a road junction. Now take the route on your left, signed to '**Magpies**' (not 'Crocker End'). You come to a sign on either side of the road to **Soundess House**. Continue ahead on this tree-lined lane towards the house, with fields either side of the lane. It ends at a cottage behind double metal gates.

② Now turn left, following the footpath sign to **Russells Water/Chilton Way Extension**. This wide path leads through woodland and passes Barnfield and Shepherds Cottage. Stay on this path until it turns to the right.

③ At this point you leave the lane and walk ahead into a field. Pass a fingerpost on your right for the 'Chiltern Way Extension'. This is a lovely stretch with

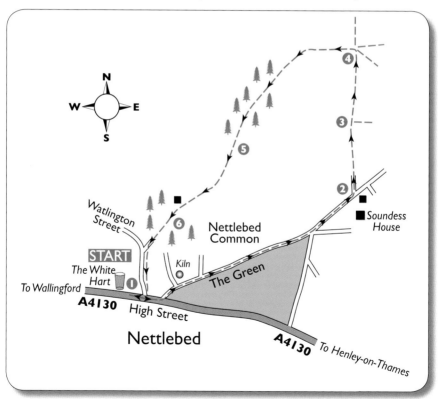

the woods of **Warburg Nature Reserve** on your right. Look out for a wooden kissing gate down on your right. Go through the gate and under some trees to a field where you will be greeted by a beautiful view across the valley. Walk along the side of the field to another kissing gate, following the signs for the Chiltern Way. In the next field, either walk diagonally, or down to the bottom, then left, to go through a kissing gate. There may be cows in this field so keep your dog close and on a lead.

Following the path at point 4 of the walk.

4 Now you are at a junction of paths. Turn left and follow the path for a short distance to a kissing gate on the left under electricity wires. Go through the gate and walk uphill a few yards to a farm gate with a smaller gate and footpath next to it. Go through the smaller gate and follow a narrow path through the woods.

5 You eventually leave the woods through a gate with a footpath sign. You are now at one end of a large field with a house in the distance. Walk ahead towards the house, stopping to admire the view behind you over the valley. Go through a gate at the side of the garden. You will need your dog on a lead now as the footpath runs by the side of a large garden. Keep to the left-hand edge of the garden and the path will lead under trees to a rough drive that leads to another house.

6 Turn left at the drive and follow it through woods for about 150 yards. When the drive veers off to the right, you need to walk ahead into the woods. The path through the trees is not very clear, but the occasional white arrow painted on a tree will reassure you that you are heading in the right direction and you are not far from Nettlebed. Walk ahead through the woods for about 65 yards, then turn half to the left, following the white arrows. After another 65 yards, you come to a crossing-path. Go over this and slightly to the right, following the arrow on a tree. Now continue ahead and you come out of the woods by some green metal gates. Turn right and walk down a track which becomes Mill Road. Pass some lovely cottages, then turn left down **Watlington Stree**t, cross the road and walk down the High Street and back to the pub.

Lewknor up to Beacon Hill

An amazing view from the top of Beacon Hill.

This is a classic Chilterns walk through a landscape of magnificent beeches, mighty oaks and chalk downland. Your dog will love sniffing about in the trees then having the wind in his ears as he emerges from the dappled woodland. You will appreciate the shade and peace of the wood and the amazing views from the top of Beacon Hill, where you can stand and watch the kites effortlessly soaring in the skies above you. An added bonus in the middle of the walk is Aston Rowant Talking Trail. Launched in 2012, there are six unique wooden sculptures with built-in audio players in the woods and on Beacon Hill. Leaflets at point 5 of the walk explain the inspiration behind each sculpture. If you have children with you they will love spotting the sculptures in the woods and pressing the buttons to hear the different voices.

The Chilterns – A Dog Walker's Guide

Terrain

A mixture of pavement, woodland tracks and paths. There are some uphill sections, but nothing too steep and there's a downhill section at the end.

Where to park

Park on the no-through-road leading to Lewknor church (GR 716976) or on the High Street near the Leathern Bottle pub. **OS Map:** Explorer 171 Chiltern Hills West.

How to get there

Leave the M40 at junction 6, take the B4009, heading towards Watlington for a few hundred yards. Then turn right down Watlington Road into Lewknor village.

Refreshments

The Leathern Bottle (otherwise known as Ye Olde Leathern Bottel) prides itself on being a dog-friendly pub where your canine companion is welcome inside and out. There is a jar of dog biscuits on the bar, a sign hanging on the door specifically welcoming dogs and a large beer garden with a children's play area in the corner. The food comes in large portions, with all the usual pub menu choices available. ☎ 01844 351482

Dog factors

Distance: 3½ miles
Road walking: About 200 yards along the pavement in Lewknor village. You also have to cross the busy B4009.
Livestock: There may be horses or sheep in some fields, so look before you let your dog off lead. Aston Rowant is a nature reserve so be extra careful about keeping your dog within sight, particularly in spring, to protect nesting birds. There are also ground nesting woodcocks in the woods.
Stiles: None
Nearest vets: Hall Place Veterinary Centre, 1A Dodds Corner, New Road, Stokenchurch HP14 3RZ ☎ 01494 485855

The Walk

1 From the pub, turn left and follow the pavement down the High Street past **Church Lane**. This Chilterns village is so charming that even the village school

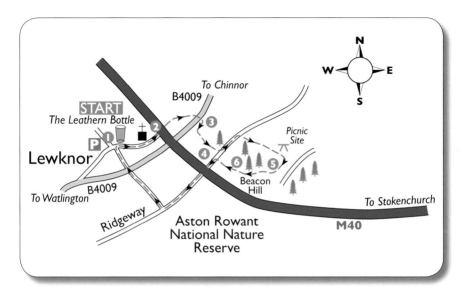

has a thatched roof. Continue out of the village to the end of the road with the M40 ahead – you can't see it but you can definitely hear it!

② Turn left here, following the footpath sign which leads you under the **M40** and across a surfaced track. Continue following the footpath through a metal swing gate and along the edge of a field to a metal gate with a white painted arrow. Turn left and walk by the side of the B4009 for a few yards until you are opposite the footpath on the other side of the road. Cross the road with care then go through a metal kissing gate into an arable field with the wooded Beacon Hill ahead of you.

③ Turn right, then left when you get to the corner, to follow the edge of the field to a wooden post with a handily painted arrow on it. Go through the gate then up, following the winding path through the trees. There are arrows painted on trees as a guide, although they are pointing back the way you came. You shortly come out of the trees onto a wide straight track – the **Ridgeway**.

④ Turn left and follow the Ridgeway until you come to the sign for **Aston Rowant National Nature Reserve**. Now turn right to follow the footpath up wooded slopes with the occasional glimpse through the trees across the Chiltern Hills. At the top of this section you come to a large beech tree with an arrow painted on it, and the footpath just beyond the tree. Turn right to follow the footpath and you might be relieved to know that that's the end of the uphill walking! You pass a picnic spot on your left, and a road and

The Leathern Bottle has welcomed walkers for 450 years.

small parking area with a wooden red kite sign welcoming you to the 'Talking Trail'.

5 Don't cross the road to continue the walk, instead do a hairpin turn to return almost the way you came, but this time following the lower path, passing an 'Aston Rowant Discovery Trail' sign. This is a wide path through beech trees, passing two sculptures. *The first sculpture you come to is 'Bat and Moth'. This represents the bats hunting for insects at Aston Rowant with the posts depicting the echolocation bats use to find insects. The second sculpture is 'From'. The small hut in the middle is for the bodgers who used to live and work in the wood making legs and spindles for chairs. When you come to the two posts forming the shelter for*

'One Ear', it shows the long ears of a brown hare. The shelter is a reference to how the hare hides its young, and the post in front represents the rare Chiltern gentian flower that grows here. Just after sculpture 2, take the left fork in the path. Go through a wooden gate into a field and walk ahead, passing 'One Ear' on your right. You are now on top of **Beacon Hill** with a wonderful view across the valley and the perfect vantage point for watching the red kites as they swoop and soar above your head. *It's worth stopping to read the noticeboard about 'The tiny yellow meadow ant farmers of Beacon Hill'. These ants are responsible for all the bumps you can see in the ground. Some of these ant-hills are over 100 years old. There is a lot going on at ground level. According to the sign, there are 20 different species of ant living on the hill and they are constantly at war with each other.* Follow the sculpture trail sign until you come to my favourite sculpture, 'The Flying Machine', inspired by the red kite. From here you have the most amazing view across the valley.

6 Walk past the sculpture to the path. *If your dog is still full of energy you could take a detour here by turning right and following the edge of the hill to see the two final sculptures, then walking back to this point.* To return to Lewknor, turn left, keeping that amazing view on your right. There is a bench along here if you have brought a picnic. When you come to a metal gate put your dog on the lead as there might be sheep in the next field. Go through the gate and, with the M40 below you and Lewknor beyond it, turn right. The path is quite narrow now and can be a bit of a scramble as you head down the field to a wooden gate, then across another field passing a sign for the Nature Reserve. Go through a metal kissing gate to the **Ridgeway**. Turn left and walk back under the motorway. When you come to a surfaced track turn right and follow the sign to **Lewknor**. At the bottom of this track, cross the road and follow the Aston Rowant Discovery Trail down a path opposite, then down concrete steps and past gardens until you see the Leathern Bottle ahead.

Bledlow and Chinnor Hill

The path across fields at the end of the walk.

This walk starts by one of my favourite pubs in the Chilterns. The 16th-century Lions of Bledlow positively welcome dogs, as well as their owners and children. In the summer months, you can watch Bledlow Village Cricket Club, with the Chinnor Steam Railway running alongside and the Chiltern Hills framing the scene. Your dog will love this wonderful walk through the woods up to Chinnor Hill Nature Reserve where you will be greeted with a stunning view across the Vale of Aylesbury. It is the perfect spot to sit, take in your surroundings and watch the kites as they soar in the sky above you. The chalk grassland is a mosaic of wild flowers in spring and summer, while the woods are filled with birdsong.

Terrain
Chinnor Hill is on sloping ground and is steep in places. The woods can be muddy after wet weather. There is up and downhill walking.

Where to park
If you are eating at the pub, there is a large car park behind it (GR 776021). Otherwise, find a spot in the village. **OS map:** Explorer 181 Chiltern Hills North.

How to get there
Bledlow is about 1 mile south-west of Princes Risborough. From the B4009, turn on to West Lane. Keep driving down the lane, under a railway bridge and past the cricket club until you get to the pub.

Refreshments
The Lions of Bledlow is very dog friendly, your pet is allowed inside or outside in the large beer garden and there's a sign on the door – *No muddy boots but muddy paws fine!* The menu is family friendly and well priced, offering half portions and spare plates for children, and there's a child menu. ☎ 01844 343345.

Dog factors

Distance: 4 miles
Road walking: None
Livestock: Horses at Wainhill Farm and there are sometimes cattle on Chinnor Hill.
Stiles: 2, both have gates for dogs.
Nearest vets: Hampden Veterinary Hospital, Haddenham Surgery, 14 Roberts Road, Haddenham, Aylesbury HP17 8HH
☎ 01296 745372

The Walk

① From the side of the pub and with the car park on your left, follow the lane gradually uphill. At the top of the lane, walk under pylons and walk ahead, following the sign 'Bridleway To Ridgeway (West)' – don't take the Chinnor Reserve path. This is a shady path with lots of blackberry bushes. At the top of the path you come to the **Ridgeway** where you turn right.

2 Now you are on higher ground with stunning views to the right across the valley and with woods either side of the path. You are soon rewarded with wonderful views glimpsed through the trees. Follow the **Ridgeway** as it winds through the trees until you come to a cottage.

3 Turn left at the cottage, leaving the Ridgeway behind, and follow the path with hedgerows on either side. Then leave the bridleway and follow the footpath past yew trees, following the sign to Chinnor Reserve. Follow the public bridleway past yew trees, now signed to **Chinnor Hill Nature Reserve**. Watch out for tree roots underfoot and continue ahead into the nature reserve. You will soon feel miles away from anywhere with only the wind in the trees for company. Pass some chalk pits on your right with an information board. Just after this, go through the swing gate on your right to

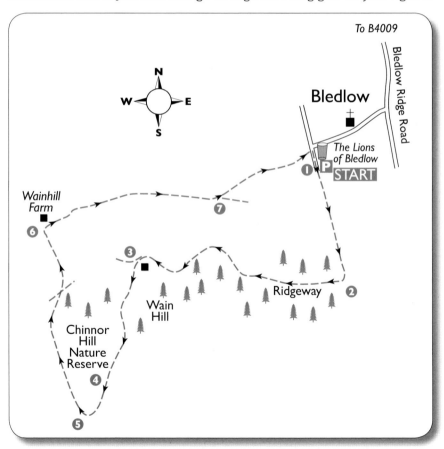

The Lions of Bledlow will make you and your hound feel welcome.

follow the permissive footpath through the reserve. Dogs need to be on leads now to protect the wildlife.

④ The path suddenly leads you out of the woods and you find yourself at the top of **Chinnor Hill** with an amazing view before you over the Vale of Aylesbury. There are even some perfectly positioned benches where you can sit and take it all in. Be aware also that there may be cattle grazing these slopes. Walk ahead along the crest of the hill, passing an information board, then go through a swing gate on the other side and down a few wooden steps to a path.

⑤ Here you turn right and walk downhill past yew trees along a sunken path. The path ends at a crossroads and a footpath sign. Cross the **Ridgeway** and follow the bridleway sign down a series of wooden steps. Continue along a path, passing a sign to show you are leaving the nature reserve on your right. When you come to a footpath turn left (don't follow the Ridgeway). Pass Ash Wain Cottage and when you come to **Wainhill Farm** turn right.

⑥ Follow the footpath past the farm buildings and across two stiles, both with dog gates. There were horses loose in the fields here while other horses watched us out of curiosity as they plodded round their horse exerciser. You are now nearly back to the start. Follow the footpath, cutting across a field, then go left along the track, until you come to the corner of another large arable field.

⑦ Turn left and cut across the field and back to the pub which you can see before you.

5

Following the Ridgeway at Pulpit Wood

The view at point 5 of the walk.

This route starts in ancient woodland with plenty of off-lead time for your dog to sniff about and explore. You then emerge from the woods to high ground on the Ridgeway, Britain's oldest road.

The woodland is filled with footpaths, as well as the Ridgeway, as it wends its way from Overton Hill and Avebury in the west to Ivinghoe Beacon in the east, following the ancient trackway that was once used by herdsmen and soldiers. There are plenty of opportunities to extend the walk, depending on how much time you have and the fitness of your dog.

You are very close to Chequers, the country retreat of the Prime Minister. You could add a mile on to the walk for a pleasant there and back stroll along the Ridgeway to the drive of Chequers. When we arrived at the pub everyone was talking about the fact that David Cameron had just been there with his family, sitting outside at one of the beer tables. This is also the pub where he accidentally left his daughter behind as everyone thought she was in someone else's car. From the car park, you could follow the signed footpath on your left uphill to the ditches and earthworks of a small Iron Age hill fort, or from the Plough, follow the Ridgeway to Whiteleaf Cross.

Terrain
Some uphill and downhill sections but nothing too steep. The bridleways in the woods can be muddy, but the path is wide so it is easy to escape the worst of the mud in the middle of the path. Once out of the woods you are on chalk downland that is easy to walk on.

Where to park
There is a free National Trust car park just off Cadsden Road at Pulpit Hill, on the left if you are driving from the Plough (GR 833046). **OS map:** 181 Chiltern Hills North

How to get there
From Askett, on the A4010 just north of Princes Risborough, follow the Cadsden Road. Pass the Plough on the right and look out for a small parking area on the left.

Refreshments
You pass the Plough in the second half of the walk. It serves delicious food, but dogs are only allowed in the beer garden in front of the pub. There is a tap to give your dog a drink, the route passes no streams so this is the only chance. The Plough is very popular with walkers and Prime Ministers, so book in advance if you want to eat.

Dog factors
· ·

Distance: 2¼ miles (you could easily extend the walk by following the Ridgeway east to the drive of Chequers, or south to Whiteleaf Hill)
Road walking: None
Livestock: None
Stiles: None
Nearest vets: Sprinz & Nash, Wellington House Veterinary Surgery, Aylesbury Rd, Princes Risborough HP27 0JP ☎ 01844 345655

The Chilterns – A Dog Walker's Guide

The Walk

1 From the car park, with your back to the road, turn right and follow the path for about 20 yards, with the road at the bottom of the bank on your right. Then at the bridleway sign on your left marked '**Icknield Way**', take the path up some wooden steps. After about 50 yards, turn left through a staggered gate onto a footpath and walk uphill through the eastern edge of **Pulpit Hill**. You can let your dog off lead here as there are no roads ahead. Now follow the narrow footpath through peaceful native woodland filled with the sound of birdsong. Pass under overhead cables and continue until you walk through a gap in the fence. There is a bridleway sign on your right and an arrow painted on the large tree in front of you.

2 Here you turn left and follow the bridleway through trees, passing a footpath sign on your right. After about ¼ mile, there is another footpath sign on your

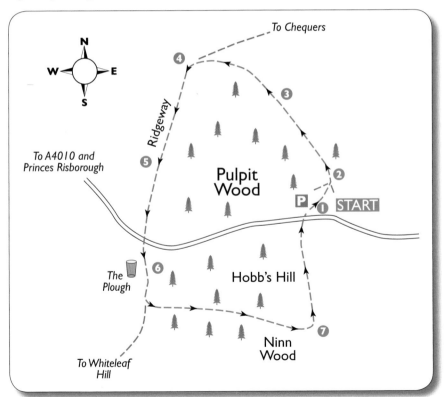

right. Turn right here to follow the path for about 10 yards to a kissing gate which you can see ahead of you.

3 Now you leave the woods to walk down a field dotted with trees and bushes and with wonderful open views towards Beacon Hill. Follow the grassy path downhill, keeping the wire fence on your right. There was a large water trough on the right when we walked here and although we saw no sign of livestock, keep your dog close until you are sure there are no sheep grazing here.

4 Shortly you come to the **Ridgeway National Trail** at the bottom of the field. Turn left and follow the Ridgeway downhill, heading west with a lovely open view across the Chilterns. *A right turn here would take you to the drive of Chequers – about ½ mile east of here. It's worth a detour if you are feeling nosy and there are some lovely views towards Coombe Hill as you walk.* You are now going to stay on the well-signed **Ridgeway** path until you get to the Plough pub. The path leads you through a metal gate and down a couple of wooden steps. Turn right to walk in the same direction along the Ridgeway as it briefly

The route takes you right past The Plough at Cadsden.

follows the route of a bridleway for a couple of yards. Then at the wooden sign, turn left and follow the Ridgeway up some wooden steps and through a kissing gate. A few more wooden steps then lead you down into a field. There are stables and paddocks down on your right and this is a wonderful spot to stop, admire the view and watch the graceful kites sweeping through the sky.

The Ridgeway has been used since prehistoric times by travellers, traders, drovers and soldiers. It provides a direct route over the drier, high ground. These people have left their mark on the landscape over time, there are Stone Age long barrows and Bronze Age sarsen stones at Avebury, Iron Age hill forts and earth banks, while thorn hedges were planted in the 18th century to contain livestock.

5 Walk down the field, following the grass path and passing a small bench on your left. Stay on the Ridgeway and walk through a metal kissing gate, cross the bridleway, then go through a wooden gate to follow the Ridgeway by the edge of the gardens of a large white house. The path ends at **Cadsden Road**, where the Ridgeway conveniently passes right in front of the Plough – a perfect spot to stop for a rest! There is a tap in the beer garden for your dog to also have a welcome drink. You can avoid this short stretch of road by turning left and walking along the edge of the wood, then cross the road and walk down to the pub.

6 Now we leave the Ridgeway to take the public footpath by the side of the beer garden, walking by the side of a double metal gate. Once more dogs can safely be off lead as there are no roads or livestock ahead. Follow the path through the woods, ignoring a footpath leading off to the right. Walk through **Ninn Wood** until the path ends at a stile, with a gap beside it that even the largest dog could easily fit through.

7 Turn left to follow the footpath sign as you return to the car park via a stretch of the **Icknield Way**. The path is fenced on either side, with fields on the right and woods on the left. However, keep in mind that the path ends on **Cadsden Road**, so as you begin to hear traffic ahead, make sure your dog is safely back on the lead. Cross the road to return to the car park.

6

Bradenham Beeches and Park Wood

Looking back towards Bradenham Manor.

The idyllic Bradenham sits quietly in a valley surrounded by beech-fringed hills. The village and surrounding woods are cared for by the National Trust who have carefully preserved this village and its many listed cottages. At the top of the large village green stands a 17th-century manor house and 14th-century church. It's a beautiful spot to while away a sunny afternoon, watching the cricket on the green in the summer, while your dog relaxes after an enjoyable romp through the surrounding woods. We met lots of friendly dog walkers as we strolled up to Park Wood, but once in the woods you will probably have the place to yourself. Almost the entire circuit is off lead, with the edges of fields and woods to sniff about in, as well as local dogs to greet, so you should have a tired and happy hound by the end of the day.

The Chilterns – A Dog Walker's Guide

Terrain
A mix of woodland paths and fields. There are some steep ascents and if you are up you know you will have to come down again shortly, but there are also some lovely views across the valley.

Where to park
There is a free National Trust car park at the south-eastern corner of Bradenham village green. From the A4010, go along Bradenham Woods Lane, first right down Rectory Lane, then first left to drive along a rough lane beside the green to the car park. Drive slowly as the lane is potholed. (GR 827970) **OS map:** Explorer 172 Chiltern Hills East.

How to get there
Bradenham is off the A4010, just north-west of West Wycombe.

Refreshments
The Red Lion is on the corner of the A4010 and Bradenham Woods Lane. Dogs are welcome in the front bar. It is open from Tuesday to Sunday and serves lunch every day and evening meals on Friday and Saturday. ☎ 01494 562212 Postcode HP14 4HF.

Dog factors
Distance: 4 miles
Road walking: About 200 yards on a quiet road with no pavements but grassy banks. You have to cross Bradenham Woods Road twice, but it is very quiet.
Livestock: Sheep at point 5.
Stiles: None
Nearest vets: Crossroads Veterinary Centre, 54 West Wycombe Road, High Wycombe HP11 2LP ☎ 01494 459095

The Walk

1 From the National Trust car park, walk across the top of the common, passing the gates of **Bradenham Manor**. *The Manor House was the home of Isaac D'Israeli. His son Benjamin Disraeli lived here as a boy, before moving to nearby Hughenden Manor as an adult when he was Queen Victoria's favourite Prime Minister.* Cross the road to a footpath signed almost directly opposite. It is a wide hedge-lined path next to Old School. Follow the path into a field and through two gates. As long as there is no livestock in the fields your dog should be fine off lead now. Keep walking, heading for the left-hand edge of **Bradenham Beeches** which you can see on top of the hill ahead of you. Cross a track and go through a metal kissing gate, then walk up the field to another gate in the top left corner of the field.

② Now walk straight on, ignoring the path on your right, to walk by the side of the wood, following the footpath uphill. Go through a kissing gate and follow a wide path, looking out for a couple of log benches on your right where you could stop for a rest and to admire the wonderful view. Follow the edge of the wood round to the left, now heading downhill and through a kissing gate.

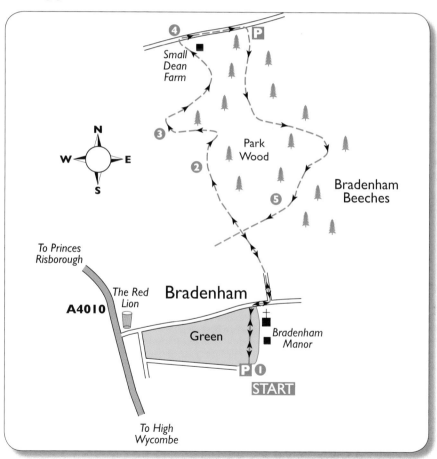

3 There is a footpath that comes from your left, turn right to follow this path through a large gap in the hedge. After about 50 yards, turn right to walk once more by the side of woods with a field on your left and **Small Dean Farm** ahead. Follow the field edge to walk past the farm, then put your dog on a lead as you walk past its barns to the road. The footpath is clearly signed and easy to follow. *Small Dean Farm is owned by the National Trust and sells ice creams, eggs, tea and coffee from the farmhouse. Look out for the 18th-century Grade II listed barn on the south side of the farmyard.*

Autumn colours in Bradenham Beeches.

4 Turn right at the road and walk for about 200 yards to a small car park on your right. Go through the car park and follow the public footpath as a sunken track leads you past the farm on your right then into Park Wood, a former Tudor deer park. Dogs are fine off lead again. Ignore a path on your left and continue ahead until you come to a choice of paths. Take the 'No Horses' path on the left which winds uphill through **Park Wood** then into Bradenham Beeches. There are various paths coming in from the left and right, but you need to follow the white arrows that are handily painted on trees, and the yellow public footpath signs. If you have children with you, spotting the arrows in the woods will keep them charging on with enthusiasm. Dogs need no added incentives to run through the woods! Eventually you walk down to a clear cross track where you turn right and walk downhill until you come to a gate with a field beyond it, there's also a footpath running up to the right here.

5 You need your dog back on a lead here as you are going through the gate into the field where there are often sheep. As you walk down the field you can see the golden ball on top of West Wycombe's St Lawrence church on the horizon ahead of you. Go through a gate on the other side of the field then follow the track between the hedgerows. Eventually you come to a strange log bench where you turn left and retrace your steps back to **Bradenham**.

Beech Woods in the Hughenden Estate

Hughenden Manor was home to Benjamin Disraeli in the 19th century.

This is a magnificent walk for your dog with almost the whole route being off lead. The woods are popular with dog walkers so there will probably be a few other hounds to meet and greet along the way. Hughenden Manor in the middle of the walk is a visual treat, and there's a café, shop and toilets in the stableyard. You are rewarded with wonderful far-reaching views across the valley as you walk through the estate, before heading back into the woods for the return leg. The changing colours of the woods through the seasons are a delight. There are bluebells in the spring when the woods are alive with birdsong, lush green foliage in the summer followed by rich autumn colours as the winter months draw near. You can see some pits in the woods, evidence of how important this area was for supplying beech wood for the chair-making industry and clay to make tiles for the local kilns.

The Chilterns – A Dog Walker's Guide

Terrain
Mainly woodland paths that can be muddy in winter. As you are walking on fallen leaves with roots and stones you would be better off wearing proper walking shoes. The path is uneven in places with some uphill stretches.

Where to park
You can park in Downley by the common, just past the Bricklayers Arms, but don't leave your car in the pub car park – there's a £20 fine! (GR 849952) **OS map:** Explorer 172 Chiltern Hills East.

How to get there
Downley is on the northern edge of High Wycombe. Coates Lane, which is off the A4128, leads you to the common.

Refreshments
Despite the fine for parking, the Bricklayers Arms is a friendly pub with painted dog footprints leading from the pavement to a dog house and water bowl at the front, where there are picnic tables for their owners to have a drink. The pub serves food and has a children's menu. ☎ 01494 452687. Postcode HP13 5XJ. At Hughenden Manor, you pass a National Trust café with picnic tables outside in the stableyard. The café is open from February to December.

Dog factors
. . . .
Distance: 4½ miles
Road walking: None
Livestock: None
Stiles: None
Nearest vets: Crossroads Veterinary Centre, 54 West Wycombe Road, High Wycombe HP11 2LP ☎ 01494 459095

The Walk
. . . .

1 From the bus stop on the western corner of the common, walk diagonally across the common, heading for the footpath post by the chapel on the other side. This is a popular route with local dog walkers and you can see where to walk as the grass has been worn down here. At the other side walk down to the path and you will find yourself by a fingerpost with a choice of paths. There are dog bins on the common and on the path in front of the chapel.

2 Don't take the path that leads to the chapel and parking area, instead, with your back to the common turn right and follow the footpath into the woods, soon passing **Well Cottage** on your left. These lovely woods are safe off-lead time. Shortly you come to a junction of paths and another fingerpost. A path on your right leads steeply up a bank, two paths lead off to your left (you will walk down one of those paths at the end of the walk), but now you need to take the path that leads straight on, passing a National Trust Hughenden Manor Farm sign on your right. Follow this path through the beechwood, then past fields with a fence on one side and a hedge on the other. You walk back into woods and stay on this path, ignoring the various side paths, as it climbs and weaves through the woods, passing another sign for Hughenden Manor. You will eventually come to a drive. You will need your dog back on a lead now. Walk ahead past the entrance to the manor house on your right and the

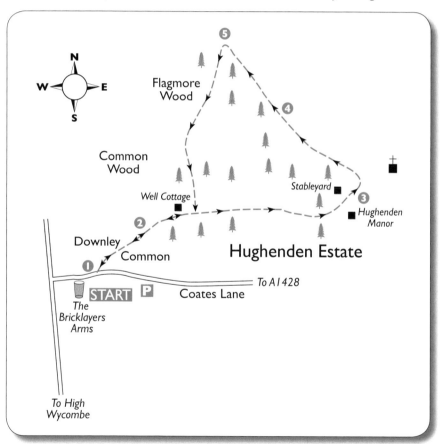

café, toilets and shop on your left in the stableyard. *Hughendon Manor was the country home of the flamboyant Benjamin Disraeli, Queen Victoria's favourite Prime Minister. He is buried in the churchyard of St Michael and All Angels, which you can see from point 3. The house was built in the mid 18th century, but after Disraeli bought it in 1848, he made many changes, removing its Georgian features in favour of a more gothic architectural style.*

③ Walk along the drive, crossing a cattle grid with a space in the middle that dogs can walk over. There are lovely views of the church and across the valley. Don't walk as far as the church, unless you want to take a quick detour to admire it. Instead, turn left and follow the public footpath signed to Naphill. Go through a metal gate and follow the path with a fence on your right. Your dog is safe off lead again. When you come to a post turn right, following the National Trust red arrow. Now stay on this undulating path as it leads through the woods to a metal gate, again with the National Trust sign.

④ Go through the gate into a field and walk ahead, with a lovely view to your right across the valley. There's another signed metal gate on the other side of the field then walk ahead by the side of an arable field with a hedge on your right. Cross a farm track and continue in the same direction, following the red National Trust arrows, with fields on either side of you and **Flagmore Wood** first ahead of you, and then on your left.

⑤ When you come to the northern tip of the wood, turn left through a metal gate and follow the footpath through the wood. When you come to a post with a '3' on it, go ahead and downhill, following the National Trust red arrows. Ignore any cross tracks and continue along the path until you eventually come to a cross track with another fingerpost and a farm gate 100 yards to your left. Turn right and follow this wide path. When you come to a footpath sign, turn left following the sign for '**Downley**'. This uphill path takes you through the woods, look out for the occasional white arrow painted on the trees. Soon you will spot a recreation field on your right through the trees. At the end of the field there is a choice of paths. Take the option on your right, passing another painted arrow as you go. When you come to a wooden swing gate, don't go through it, instead turn left and walk downhill. You will shortly find yourself at a junction of paths with the Hughenden Manor Farm sign in front of you – the same spot that you passed at the start of the walk. Turn right and retrace your steps, passing **Well Cottage** and crossing the common to return to your car.

Exploring West Wycombe's Hills and Woods

A wonderful view on a summer's day.

This walk explores the woods and hills to the west of the National Trust village of West Wycombe. From the higher points there are magnificent views across this rolling landscape to the Dashwood Mausoleum and the church of St Lawrence with its famous tower topped by a golden ball on West Wycombe Hill.

There are some hills on this walk, but they are in the first half when you and your dogs are ready for the challenge! When you are up on the Chiltern Hills you can hear nothing but the call of the magnificent red kite as it soars on the thermals. The second half of the walk follows dappled shade through tranquil native woods. Look out for the magnificent ancient yews in the woods near West Wycombe Hill.

Arable fields and woodland give your dog plenty of opportunities to sniff about and explore off lead. I did this walk with two energetic Labradors and my whippet and they all had a wonderful time and slept for the rest of the afternoon.

The footpaths have been well maintained by the farmers, with a ruler-straight strip across most fields making the route easy to navigate. Arrows painted on some of the trees help keep you on the right track through the woodland.

Terrain

Unsurfaced paths across arable fields and through woods. There is uphill walking in the first half of the walk.

Where to park

There is a large free car park on the left as you head up Chorley Road, signed from West Wycombe (GR 826947). **OS map:** Explorer 172 Chiltern Hills East.

How to get there

From High Wycombe, take the A40 to West Wycombe. Chorley Road is at the western edge of the village.

Dog factors

Distance: 3 miles
Road walking: At the start along a pavement, and there are a couple of quiet lanes to cross in the middle of the walk.
Livestock: None
Stiles: Three at point 3 of the walk. To avoid them, you could turn right at Chorley farmhouse and follow the road back to the car park, but I did this walk with two Labradors and they managed the stiles with ease, either jumping over them like stairs, or wriggling through gaps beside them.
Nearest vets: Crossroads Veterinary Centre, 54 West Wycombe Road, High Wycombe HP11 2LP ☎ 01494 459095

Refreshments

The George and Dragon on the High Street in West Wycombe is a Grade II listed coaching inn that serves food from breakfast and snacks, through to lunch, afternoon tea and dinner. It is very dog friendly and your hound is welcome inside and out in the garden. ☎ 01494 535340, postcode HP14 3AB.

The Walk

. . . .

1 From the car park, turn right and walk down **Chorley Road** to the junction. Then turn right down **Oxford Road**, noting 'The Pound' on your right. Follow the pavement for about 150 yards until you come to a public footpath sign on the right. The path ahead is beautifully clear as the farmer has left a neat path leading diagonally across the field. The path leads you gradually uphill, but not too steeply and you are soon rewarded with lovely views of the surrounding wooded hills and the Dashwood Mausoleum on top of West

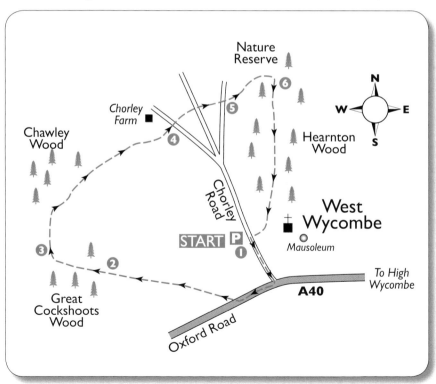

Wycombe Hill. Stop at the top of the hill to look back, catch your breath and admire the view! Beneath the hill is a network of caves that were the rumoured meeting place for the 18th-century Hellfire Club.

2 Follow the path into **Great Cockshoots Wood**. The entrance is marked with a footpath sign and there's a white arrow painted on a tree trunk. You will now be in lovely dappled shade under the beech trees. Walk through the woods and at the other side of the wood you come to a path crossing your route.

3 Turn right and follow the footpath heading north. Pass painted arrows either side of the path and continue ahead, with a large arable field on your left and trees on your right. Ahead you can see **Chawley Wood**. When you get to the edge of this wood, turn right to follow the bridleway. The path leads you past the wood, then past hedges with fields either side as you walk gradually downhill. Look out for the odd glimpse of the mausoleum on your right as you walk. At the end of this path, turn left and walk down to **Hatch Lane** and Chorley farmhouse.

4 You now need to cross the first of three roads with stiles to access the field. Follow the footpath sign, over the stile and across a short stretch of arable field with the path clearly running across the middle of it. At the other side of the field the next stile also has a gate. Cross **Foxboro Hill** with care as it is a fast road. The dogs jumped over this stile to cross into the next arable field. You can now see the wooded hill rising up ahead of you and West Wycombe on your right. There is a stile at the edge of this field, but with a gap next to it for dogs. Cross **Slough Lane** with another stile and a gap by it for dogs.

5 Now you reach the only part of the walk where the footpath has not been maintained. There is about 200 yards of public footpath directly ahead of you between the fields with a gate at the end of it into the woods. In high summer this narrow tunnel becomes completely overgrown with nettles. It is the only way into the beautiful woodland ahead of you, so walkers have found their way round this by walking up the edge of the field on the left. At the top of the footpath there is a gap in the hedge where you can join the path for the last few yards where it's less overgrown and so reach the gate into the woods. The path now veers to the left and leads you steeply uphill, but there are some wooden steps to help you along the path. At the top you are rewarded with a magnificent view and a well-positioned bench. There's even a trough so your dog can have a drink.

6 Go through the gate into the welcome shade of **Hearnton Wood**. There are more wooden steps here and arrows on the trees to reassure you that you are heading in the right direction. You come to a cross path with a painted arrow

Stopping for a rest in the shade.

on the tree. Now turn right and follow a wider, rutted track. As you walk you pass a National Trust sign on the right for '**West Wycombe Hill**'. This shady track is a pleasure to walk along on a hot day. Eventually you come to a wooden fingerpost and a footpath sign. Turn right to follow the narrower path downhill. There is an arrow painted on a tree halfway down this path. Go through a staggered fence and pass some magnificent ancient yews on your left. If you have children with you they will find climbing these trees hard to resist! When you begin to hear traffic ahead, you come to a narrow path leading down to the road. Make sure your dog is safely back on the lead and walk down to the road. The car park is opposite you.

Roald Dahl's Great Missenden and the Surrounding Woodland

Walking downhill towards Great Missenden at point 5.

The delightful village of Great Missenden in the heart of the Chilterns was home to the celebrated author Roald Dahl for 36 years and the surrounding landscape was the inspiration for some of his popular children's books. This walk takes you right past his home, Gipsy House, which is still owned by the Dahl family. He chose to write his books in a special hut in the garden. The contents of the hut have all been moved to the museum where it has been lovingly recreated. While your dog can have some safe off-lead time sniffing about in Hobbshill Wood, if he suddenly races off it might not be a squirrel that he's spotted. Dahl walked with his children in these woods and he would entertain them with stories. His last book, *The Minbins* tells of a 'Red-Hot Smoke-Belching Gruncher' who lived in the woods. It is a typically dark tale as the Gruncher grunches up everything in its way. As you walk back to the village the views across the Misbourne Valley are spectacular. The Chiltern Hills are cloaked with beech trees and in early autumn as the colours begin to change the effect is stunning. A stroll along Great Missenden High Street brings you back to the car, passing independent shops, an award-winning museum and two dog-friendly pubs along the way.

Terrain
The first stretch of the walk is along a surfaced lane, perfect for the wetter months. Once under the shade of the woods it is muddier, but the path is wide so you can normally pick your way round the worst patches. The second half of the walk is level, then downhill along grass paths.

Where to park
The pay and display car park on Link Road is free on Sundays. It is clearly signed from the High Street as the recommended parking for the Roald Dahl Museum (GR 895014). **OS map:** Explorer 181 Chiltern Hills North.

How to get there
Great Missenden is off the A413 between Amersham and Wendover. There are brown tourist signs directing you to the parking.

Refreshments
There are two pubs on the High Street in Great Missenden and both allow dogs in the beer garden. The Cross Keys (☎ 01494 865373) is a traditional pub with a beer garden and a fantastic range of puddings baked by the landlady. The White Lion (☎ 01494 863696) serves tapas.

Dog factors
. . . .

Distance: 2½ miles
Road walking: Some pavement walking in Great Missenden and country lanes where there might be cyclists.
Livestock: None but the route passes paddocks, and there could be horse riders on the bridleway.
Stiles: None
Nearest vets: Wheelhouse Veterinary Centre, Amersham Road, Chesham HP5 1NQ ☎ 01494 782001, or Wheelhouse Veterinary Centre, 1 Woodside Close, Amersham HP6 5EG ☎ 01494 725320

The Chilterns – A Dog Walker's Guide

The Walk

1 Turn right out of the car park and walk up to the High Street. Cross the High Street, turn right passing the post office, then left to walk up **Station Approach**. You walk over the railway lines then turn left down **Trafford Road**.

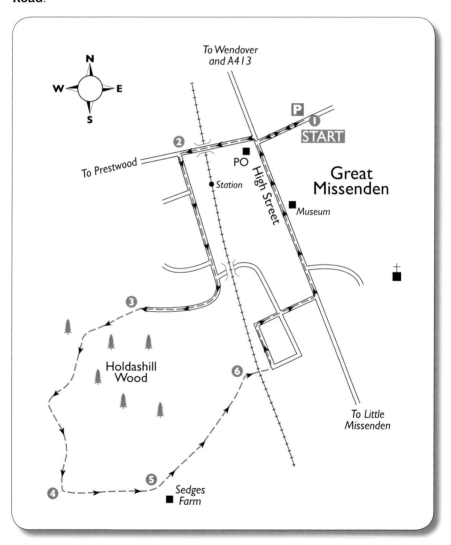

Great Missenden's petrol pumps inspired the description of the garage in
Danny the Champion of the World.

*The small post office once delivered around 4,000 letters a week to Roald Dahl.
The author wrote a* Poem to School Children *in 1986, thanking them for all the
letters. It starts: 'Dear children, far across the sea, how good of you to write to
me … ', and ends: 'Young people, and I think I'm right, Are nicer when they're
out of sight.'*

2 There are a lot of 'Private' signs at this point, but there is also a 'public footpath' sign so march along without any worries. As you walk past the houses you glimpse between their garages the most amazing view that they have from their back gardens. At the end of the road turn right to follow a country lane. Pass the gates of a garden centre on your left, then the walls of **Gipsy House** on your right. The lane now leads you uphill between tall hedgerows. There are sheep in the fields on your left but they are securely fenced off.

3 At the top of the lane turn left and follow the bridleway first along a surfaced track, then, as you pass **Angling Spring Farm**, the bridleway continues directly ahead along a mud track. The path is fenced on either side so your dog is quite safe to sniff about. The path passes a 'Wildlife Conservation Area' on your right. Continue heading slightly downhill through the woods, where the path veers to the left at the bottom and the woodland opens up with a large arable field on the right.

4 At the end of the path you come to a surfaced lane. You will need your dog under close control now and be aware that the area is popular with horse riders. Turn left to follow the path by a drive lined with trees with paddocks on either side. Soon you will be able to see Great Missenden church on your left, surrounded by trees. Stay on the footpath as you go through a large wooden gate and approach **Sedges Farm**.

5 When you come to the buildings, the footpath is clearly signed with a left turn. Walk down the valley towards the village enjoying the stunning view.

6 When you come to a gate on your right, go through it and over the railway on a footbridge. Turn right through a kissing gate and you will find yourself among houses on the edge of the village. Take the first left down **Hobbshill Road**, then turn right and walk down to the **High Street**, where you turn left to return to your car.

If you have children with you then to walk past The Roald Dahl Museum and Story Centre without paying a visit would be a shame. This original and creative museum has interactive galleries with an emphasis on story telling and the imagination. It is for children not dogs so one adult would have to either follow another walk, Little Missenden is very close by, or if your dog has short legs, sit and wait in one of the pubs!

Water and Woods at Little Missenden

Looking back to admire Little Missenden at the start of the walk.

You and your hound will love this stroll – it has everything you could look for in a Chilterns walk. Starting with a splendid view across the Misbourne valley, you cross large arable fields where your dog can stretch his legs, then woods to sniff about in, before a leisurely return by the banks of the river Misbourne. These meadows are popular with local dog walkers so be prepared for lots of meeting and greeting. In the middle of the walk you pass a cricket green and the immaculately maintained 'Field of Remembrance', a community project to remember the fallen during the Great War. Little Missenden and its Saxon church are well worth exploring if you have time at the end of the walk. And if you are puzzled as to why this very English village looks strangely familiar to you, *Midsomer Murders* and *Miss Marple* have both been filmed here.

The Chilterns – A Dog Walker's Guide

Terrain
There is an ascent at the start of the walk, but nothing too strenuous, then downhill on the second half of the walk as you return through woods to a stretch of easy walking along the Misbourne valley.

Where to park
There is space roadside near the Crown Inn (HP7 0RD) but pull in as much as possible and avoid blocking gates (GR 926988). **OS map:** Explorer 172 Chiltern Hills East.

How to get there
Turn south off the A413 Amersham to Aylesbury road and follow a minor road to Little Missenden.

Refreshments
The walk starts by the Crown Inn (☎ 01494 862571). They serve food from Monday to Saturday from 12 pm to 2 pm. Dogs are welcome in the beer garden and you can park in their car park if you are also eating in the pub. The Red Lion has a beer garden that backs onto the river and welcomes dogs inside and out (☎ 01494 862876).

Dog factors
. . . .

Distance: 4½ miles
Road walking: None
Livestock: There may be sheep in the fields and you pass close to Mop End Farm.
Stiles: Some stiles but with gaps for dogs.
Nearest vets: Wheelhouse Veterinary Centre, Amersham Road, Chesham HP5 1NQ ☎ 01494 782001 or Wheelhouse Veterinary Centre, 1 Woodside Close, Amersham HP6 5EG ☎ 01494 725320

The Walk
. . . .

1 With your back to the Crown Inn, take the public bridleway in front of you next to the village hall, signed 'Chiltern Heritage Trail', passing **Toby's Lane Farm**. Continue ahead and slightly uphill, it is safe to have your dog off-lead here. The path leads steadily uphill, but the views across the valley make the climb more than worthwhile. Stay on this path, walking with a wood on your right, following the public bridleway and a blue arrow. When the wood ends, follow the path for about 250 yards, then just before the path curves slightly to the right, go through the wooden gate on your left.

2 You will now find yourself at the edge of a large arable field. The footpath leads diagonally ahead and to the right across the field, and then in the same direction across the next field. Head for the pylons if you are unsure. When you get to the other side of the field, turn right at the footpath post and follow the path beside a hedge and under the large electricity pylons. The path becomes a track, leading to **Mop End Farm**, and you will need to have your dog back on a lead now.

3 Cross the stile on your left into the field, there are plenty of gaps in the fence for your dog. Then cross the field aiming just to the left of the farm buildings

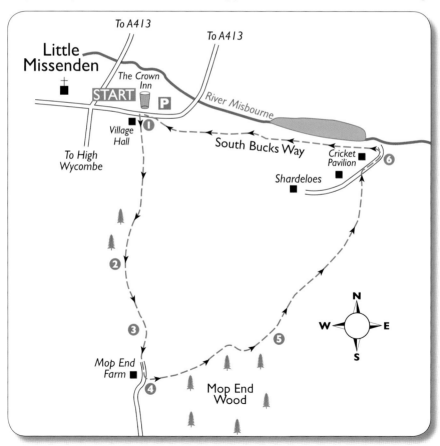

where there is a stile half hidden in the hedge taking you out of this field. The last time I walked past here there was the sound of lots of barking, then as I climbed over the stile a collie, followed by a terrier with a German shepherd close behind came tearing towards me across the farmyard. I must admit I was rather worried, but like many farm dogs they were well trained and knew to stop at the invisible line where the farmyard stopped and the track began, even with the gate wide open. Walk down the lane away from the farm and very soon there is a footpath sign on your left into lovely woods.

4 Now enjoy some safe off-lead time as you follow the path winding its way downhill through the trees. Eventually you come to a gap in a fence with a stile on your right. Here you walk ahead into a large sloping field. You will need your dog back on a lead as there can be sheep here.

5 Walk ahead across this large field and at the other side continue ahead along a track. When you come to a fork in the path, bear left and walk with a line of large trees on your right. Soon you will see a large cream house ahead of you. The path eventually leads you to the drive to **Shardeloes** and **Lower Park House**. Turn right and walk down the drive, passing a cricket green.

6 At the bottom of this track, just before West Lodge, turn left to follow the **South Bucks Way** along a surfaced track. *Behind the cricket pavilion there is a striking Field of Remembrance with rows of white crosses. Each cross represents 50,000 men and women who died in the First World War.* With the Field of Remembrance on your left and the pavilion behind you, walk to a gap in the fence signed South Bucks Way. Now follow this path by sweeping green meadows and the lake and river back to **Little Missenden**. The meadows are divided by gates. Watch out as there can be sheep in the fields. There are also lots of local dog walkers so a sociable time is had by all.

The impressive house you can see up on your left is Shardeloes. It was a haven for expectant mothers during the Second World War when it was used as a maternity home. The peace of the Chilterns was considered more conducive to an easy birth than bombs and the Blitz!

Meeting friendly dog walkers on the South Bucks Way.

Coleshill Village on top of the Chiltern Hills

Coleshill Village Pond is an idyllic picnic spot.

Nestled on a hilltop is the picture-perfect village of Coleshill. It has a church, pub, pond, a common that has been open land since the Middle Ages and even a windmill. There are some gorgeous cottages and gardens to admire as you stroll along the quiet lanes, and the bench by the pond is a peaceful spot to sit and watch the world go by on a fine summer's day. From the village, your dog can stretch his legs as you cross large arable fields to woodland, before returning past the church to the village.

The Chilterns – A Dog Walker's Guide

Terrain
There is some road walking in the village but the roads are very quiet and popular with walkers. Field and woodland paths could be muddy in wet weather. There is some uphill walking, but nothing too strenuous.

Where to park
You can park in the Red Lion car park if you are eating there but they ask that you check with the landlord first. Otherwise, find a spot roadside, making sure that you don't block a drive (GR 948952). **OS Map:** Explorer 172 Chiltern Hills East.

How to get there
On the A335 about 2 miles south of Amersham there is a right turn to Coleshill. Follow this winding road into the village, ignoring a right turn on New Road.

Refreshments
The Red Lion (☎ 01494 727020) is a friendly village pub with a beer garden and children's play area. Dogs are welcome on a lead and lunch is served daily from 12 noon to 2.25 pm. Evening meals are served on Monday to Saturday from 7 pm to 9 pm.

Dog factors

Distance: 2½ miles
Road walking: There is road walking in the villages but the roads are quiet with grass verges.
Livestock: The fields are arable so there is no livestock but in the woods there are lots of game birds so keep your dog in sight and on a lead if you are near the birds.
Stiles: None
Nearest vets: Straid Veterinary Clinic, 121 Station Road, Beaconsfield HP9 1LH ☎ 01494 673101

The Walk

1 From the Red Lion, turn left and walk down **Village Road**, passing the large pond. Continue until the point where the road turns into **Windmill Hill**. Turn right here to follow a short grassy path onto **Coleshill Common**. Your dog will love exploring the common so take your time in this lovely spot, but keep

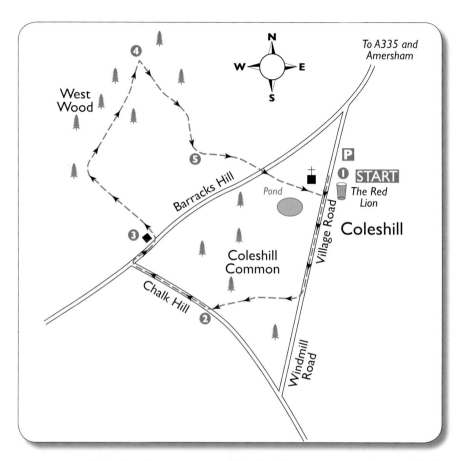

an eye on which direction you are walking in. You want to end up on Chalk Hill, so follow the path into a large open area, cross this, passing a large oak tree on your right. Then walk ahead through the trees and across a small plank bridge to **Chalk Hill**.

② Turn right and walk downhill to a junction where you turn right again onto **Barracks Hill**. The footpath you need is next to the first house on the left. Walk past the house then turn left and follow the footpath into a large arable field.

③ The point you need to aim for is the right edge of the wood that you can see ahead of you on the other side of the field. Depending on the time of year and the state of the crop, either walk ahead or round the edge of this large field. There is a footpath sign at the entrance to the wood and a gap in the trees. These beech woods are private but with public footpaths running through them and depending on the season, there could be lots of game birds so keep an eye on your dog and if you think he is likely to chase them keep him on a lead. The footpath you need is almost directly on your right. Follow this path as it meanders through the woods.

4 The path ends at a T junction, with a gate a few yards down on your left and a field beyond that. Don't go through the gate, instead turn right and walk slightly uphill. Follow the path through these lovely woods, following the public footpath signs. As the path curves round to the right, stay on the path as it leads you out of the woods and into a field, passing a white arrow on the fence. Continue in the same direction with a fence on your left until you come to a gate.

5 Turn left and walk through the gate. You are now at the edge of **Coleshill** and as you follow the grassy track you will soon find yourself passing gardens as the track changes to a surfaced lane and leads you to the church. Cross the road to follow the path by the side of the church and you will find yourself opposite the pub.

The Red Lion offers a warm welcome to thirsty walkers.

Cholesbury Iron Age Camp and Common

The impressive defences of the Iron Age fort at point 4.

On a ridge of the Chilterns are the hilltop villages of Cholesbury and Hawridge and to the east of the Cholesbury to Chesham Road is common land. This lovely walk follows a mosaic of lush green meadows, flowery grassland, scrub and woodland to the impressive earthworks of Cholesbury Iron Age Camp. The ancient ramparts are surrounded by magnificent beech trees and it's a peaceful spot to walk through. The return takes you across part of Cholesbury and Hawridge Common, which is a very popular spot with dog walkers so your pet is sure to make some friends.

The Chilterns – A Dog Walker's Guide

Terrain
After an initial stretch by the side of a road, the rest of this walk follows field paths and woods, before ending on the flat grass of the common.

Where to park
There is a layby at the side of the Common, just next to the Full Moon pub (GR 935070) **OS map:** Explorer 181 Chiltern Hills North.

How to get there
Cholesbury is between Chesham and Tring. Take the A416 out of Chesham and turn left on Vale Road signed to Hawridge and Cholesbury. Continue to the Full Moon in Cholesbury.

Refreshments
The Full Moon is a family friendly pub with an outside seating area. It serves home-cooked food and is open every day. ☎ 01494 758959

Dog factors
Distance: 2½ miles
Road walking: Rays Hill has no pavements but is a wide road with grass verges so it is easy to get out of the way of the occasional car that might pass.
Livestock: There are sometimes sheep in the meadows at the start of the walk.
Stiles: There are stiles on this walk, but all with gaps for dogs to get through. I didn't have to lift my dog over any of the stiles.
Nearest vets: Springwell Veterinary Surgery, 98 Western Road, Tring, Hertfordshire HP23 4BJ ☎ 01442 822151

The Walk

1 From the parking spot, turn left down **Ray's Hill**. After a few yards you will spot Cholesbury's windmill. Walk down the side of this road, there are no pavements but it is wide with grass verges and little traffic. When the road turns to the left there are footpath posts on either side of the road. Turn right and follow the public footpath. There's a farmer's gate with a gap next to it for walkers and dogs, then another gate with a stile next to it, but you can open the gate if necessary to get your dog through. Now walk ahead along a valley bottom by lush green meadows divided by a series of gates or stiles

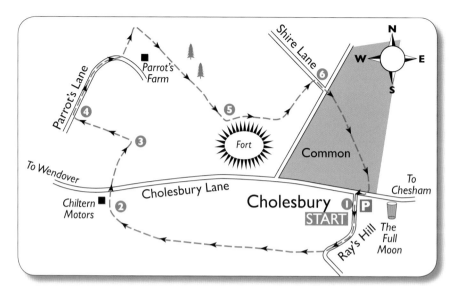

with gaps for dogs. Be aware that there could be sheep in these meadows, so check before letting your dog off lead. When you come to an electricity pole go forward to the far right corner of the next field. From a kissing gate in the corner, go ahead along the right-hand edge of two arable fields with a hedge on your right.

2 You come to a row of Scots pines where you turn right and follow a narrow path by the side of **Chiltern Motors**. Note their vintage petrol pumps – 4s.11d. per quart! Cross the road and take the footpath opposite, by the side of a large metal gate. The path takes you through a kissing gate and into a large field planted with oak trees. Look for a left turning in the field after about 20 yards and go through a kissing gate in the hedge, then turn right and head for another gate at the far corner of a field planted with trees. Go through the kissing gate.

3 Then turn left and go through another gate by a bench, as though you might be going back on yourself. You can see where walkers have crossed this field. Follow the grass path heading for the far right corner. There is a stile at the other side with space for dogs to get through, but the next field is a paddock so make sure your pet is safely back on a lead now. Head left across the paddock, then follow a narrow path which leads you to **Parrott's Lane**.

4 This lane has grassy verges rather than pavements but is very quiet. Turn right and follow the lane as it dips up and down until you come to the double wooden gates of **Parrott's Farm**. There is a gate to the left of the farm with a rather rickety stile. Cross the stile and the next meadow to another stile which leads you into beautiful native woodland. Now you turn right and follow the path at the edge of the woods for about 100 yards to a kissing gate on your right. Go through the gate and across the right-hand edge of the next meadow, walking through trees and two kissing gates. Then walk ahead through the trees and under electricity lines to come to the impressive embankments of the Iron Age **Cholesbury Camp**. *Cholesbury Camp, excavated in 1932, was occupied in the 2nd and 1st centuries BC although pottery found at the site shows that it was in use before this date, and continued to be used into the Roman period. The bank rises in a 'v' shape to 13 ft above the bottom of the ditch and there are signs of a second ditch that was dug but not completed. There is a noticeboard here explaining how it once looked.*

An enthusiastic walking companion.

5 Turn left and follow the bank. Walk for a time enjoying this peaceful spot. Eventually you come to a crossing with a field ahead with a closely cut lawn. Turn left and walk a short distance with the field then houses on your right until you come to **Shire Lane**.

6 Turn right at the road and walk to a T junction. Then leave the road behind and follow the path straight ahead of you across **Cholesbury Common**. At the first junction of paths take the route on your right then walk across the common looking out for little painted white men on posts to show you are heading in the right direction. Soon you will spot the cricket green then continue ahead to your car.

Waterside Walking by the Wendover Arm

The walk starts by the Wendover Arm.

The shady towpath by the Wendover Arm winds its way along the bottom of the Chiltern Hills to the Tring summit of the Grand Union Canal. This waterside walk follows a section of the canal with the occasional view across the fields towards the monument on Coombe Hill and Wendover Woods. The second half of the walk heads off across the fields to pass the medieval church of St Mary the Virgin at Weston Turville, before passing the dog-friendly Village Gate pub to return across more fields to picturesque Wendover.

The Chilterns – A Dog Walker's Guide

The Wendover Arm is an ideal option for dog walkers on a hot summer's day. You are under the cool of the trees and right by the water for your hound to have a swim and a drink, and you will meet lots of other dogs by the canal. You could adapt this walk to a simple there and back by following the Wendover Arm to Halton, or explore even further by following the footpath to Halton, then heading west into Wendover Woods.

Terrain
Level walking. The ease of walking across the fields will depend on the season, in high summer the grass on the footpaths around Church Farm can grow tall.

Where to park
Park roadside on Wharf Road in Wendover, being careful not to block residents' drives. (GR 868082) **OS map:** Explorer 181 Chiltern Hills North.

How to get there
Wendover is south of Aylesbury on the A413. At the World's End roundabout take the first left on to the B4009 (Wendover Road) then turn left on to Wharf Road.

Refreshments
The Village Gate on the Aylesbury Road welcomes dogs in the bar area and has a beer garden. It serves food all day and there's a water bowl in the garden for your hound. ☎ 01296 623884.

Dog factors
Distance: 4 miles
Road walking: A short stretch along a pavement in the middle of the walk and some residential streets in Wendover at the end.
Livestock: There are plenty of ducks and swans on the canal. Sheep and cows may be in some of the fields so keep your dog on a lead when you enter a field until you are sure it's safe.
Stiles: There is a one stile at Church Farm but there is a space under it for dogs to fit through.
Nearest vets: Wendover Heights Veterinary Centre, 1 Tring Road, Halton, Aylesbury HP22 5PN ☎ 01296 623439, or Hampden Veterinary Hospital, Elm Farm Surgery, 2 Elm Court, Elm Farm Road, Aylesbury HP21 7NQ ☎ 01296 745370

The Walk

1 The public footpath sign leading you from **Wharf Road** down to the canal is next to house number 41. The path leads you down to the canal, a

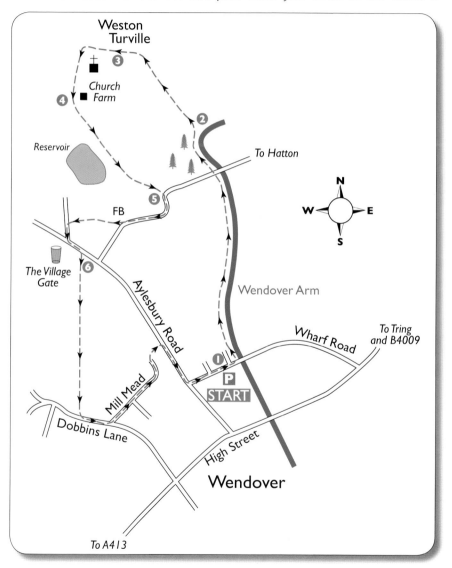

conveniently placed dog waste bin and an information sign telling you the history of the canal. Now follow the path ahead, with the canal on your right. There is no fence initially on your left, so for the first 100 yards or so keep your dog on a lead to stop it running into the road or someone's garden. Soon you leave Wendover behind and follow the sleepy canal past woods and meadows with just the ducks for company. *The Wendover Arm was built in the late 1790s to bring water from a natural spring at Wellhead near St Mary's church in Wendover to the Tring summit of the Grand Union Canal. Water from the Coombe and Boddington hills meets at the Wellhead and this water was diverted from a natural stream to form the Wendover Arm. Keeping a canal full at high points was a constant challenge for the 18th-century engineers. The Wendover Arm Trust was formed in 1989 with the aim to restore this stretch of water to make it fully navigable.* When you pass two benches on your right and a very narrow footbridge, this is the spot where the railway line once cut across the canal. Continue walking and pass under **Perch Bridge**, marked 'WA 10'. There is another dog waste bin here. Walk through a wooded area and look out for a public footpath sign.

2 Now we leave the canal behind. Turn left to follow the footpath through a kissing gate and walk by the side of a large arable field towards Weston Turville. When you come to a choice of paths, ignore the bridleway on your right, instead follow the footpath through a metal kissing gate then follow the grassy path diagonally across the field. The farmer has put signs up here asking that you keep dogs on leads and when I walked this way there were cows in the next field with an electric fence that would keep a cow in, but a dog could easily fit underneath it.

3 At the end of the field, go through the kissing gate into **St Mary's** churchyard. This medieval church dates back to the 13th century and has a 15th-century tower and roof. There is a gravestone, on the left as you enter the churchyard, for 19-year-old Private H L Kempster from the Oxford and Bucks Light Infantry who was killed in the First World War. Follow the

Walking through St Mary's churchyard in Weston Turville at point 3.

path across the churchyard and through the lychgate to the road, where there is another dog waste bin. Walk ahead to the public footpath sign on the left, by the driveway to **Church Farm**.

4 The farmer has marked the route of the footpath with occasional white posts, although the walk is easy to navigate. Go through the metal kissing gate and follow the edge of the field and walk past the farmhouse to a stile – with a space under it that even a large dog could fit through. You are now on the edge of arable fields and over to the right you can see the raised banks of the Weston Turville reservoir. Walk ahead between two fields with a view of Wendover Woods on the horizon ahead of you. At the end of this field you pass another white post and an old harrow. Follow the sign for Weston Turville and walk through some trees for about 100 yards. *There is a sign on your right for a nature reserve, a short detour down this path takes you to a remote bird hide.* But for the walk continue ahead, pass some houses then a gate leads you out of the woods and to a parking area on **Halton Lane**, where your dog will need to be back on a lead.

5 Cross the road and turn right to follow the pavement, passing a sign about 'Halton's Heritage'. A few yards past the **Halton** village sign, cross the road again to follow the footpath on the right that leads you along a raised path by the side of the road. You can spot the monument on Coombe Hill on your left. When you come to some wooden steps on your left, follow the steps and cross a footbridge over a small stream. Then cross the field heading for the gap in the hedge on the other side of the field. Turn left and walk down to the Village Gate pub, crossing the road with care. As you face the pub, turn left and walk towards the sign for Wendover, but before you get to the sign take the footpath on your right by a house.

6 This narrow path can get overgrown in summer, but it is only for about 200 yards until a metal swing gate leads you into a large field. Walk ahead, then through another metal swing gate to a large field where there can be sheep. Cross to the far corner, then through the kissing gate and turn left down a farm track to **Dobbins Lane**. Follow this pleasant tree-lined road and turn left down **Mill Mead**. There is an eco house with a grass roof on the right towards the end of this road, and on the left is the public footpath sign. Follow the footpath past a windmill to **Aylesbury Road**. Cross the road at the pedestrian crossing and turn right. Pass Wendover Health Centre then turn left down **Wharf Road** to your car.

Coombe Hill and Wonderful Wendover

The view from Coombe Hill at point 5 of the walk.

You can't walk in the Chilterns without a trip up Coombe Hill to admire the sweeping views from the top. At 852 ft above sea level, this is one of the highest spots in the Chilterns, and with the large Grade II listed war memorial on top, it is also one of the most iconic landmarks in the area. My dog had fun on the way up attempting and failing to catch the squirrels, as despite his best efforts he couldn't follow them up a tree trunk. There were a few other dog walkers on the hill and lots of space for dogs to run around, while their owners can stop and take in the amazing view. You can spot the Prime Minister's country retreat of Chequers from the top. This land was once all part of the Chequers estate, until the government handed it over to the National Trust in the 1920s. As you walk down you keep the stunning prospect with 'the three hundreds of Aylesbury' stretched out before you. The Ridgeway then leads you through the small market town of Wendover, past thatched cottages and friendly pubs with beer gardens. Follow the Heron Path by a stream then back to the start of the walk.

Terrain

There are tree roots in the woods and the bridleway can be muddy but the ascent is gentle, so although you are travelling uphill, it isn't difficult. There is a downhill section on the return.

Where to park

Wendover Cricket Club has a car park next to it which is popular with walkers. If there is a cricket match on, then park roadside on the Witchell cul-de-sac, avoiding people's drives (GR 868078). **OS map:** Explorer 181Chiltern Hills North.

How to get there

Take the A413 and head for a roundabout at the southern end of Wendover. Turn onto London Road which then becomes South Street, then turn right onto Witchell.

Refreshments

Depending on how you time the walk, there are two pub options. The traditional King and Queen is at the start of the walk. It welcomes dogs, has a beer garden and serves food all day ☎ 01296 623272. When you come down from Coombe Hill and walk into Wendover, you pass the 18th-century Shoulder of Mutton on your left which also has a beer garden and serves food all day ☎ 01296 623223. Another good option would be to bring a picnic as there are few finer spots than at the top of Coombe Hill.

Dog factors
· ·

Distance: 3¼ miles
Road walking: The start of the walk follows a quiet country lane while the end of the walk takes you through Wendover. Dogs would have to be on a lead at these times.
Livestock: There are horses in the field at point 2.
Stiles: 2 (but with gaps so dogs don't need to cross the actual stiles)
Nearest vets: Wendover Heights Veterinary Centre, 1 Tring Road, Halton, Aylesbury HP22 5PN ☎ 01296 623439 or Elm Farm Surgery, 2 Elm Court, Elm Farm Road, Aylesbury HP21 7NQ ☎ 01296 745370

The Chilterns – A Dog Walker's Guide

The Walk

1 From Witchell, turn left down **South Street**, cross the road and walk up **Bacombe Lane**, following the Icknield Way Rider's Route. There are no pavements, but this is a very quiet country lane. Walk over the Bacombe Lane bridge. The lane narrows with a row of lovely detached houses to admire on your left, and a hedgerow then fields on your right. This is a good spot for watching the kites as they circle in the sky above you.

2 Just before '**Cedar House**', and with a wooden gate in sight at the end of the lane ahead, turn right and cross a stile (there is a space for dogs next to the stile). Check before entering the field as there were two horses here the last time I passed, but they were very friendly and fine with dogs. Follow the footpath up towards the stile that you can see opposite you. As you walk up the field, look to your right to catch a glimpse of the impressive Waddesdon Manor.

3 Cross the stile (this time with a special dog gate) and you are now in the woods and dogs can be safely off-lead. Turn left to follow the bridleway. The route isn't too steep, but does gradually lead you uphill. Pass a 'Walkers

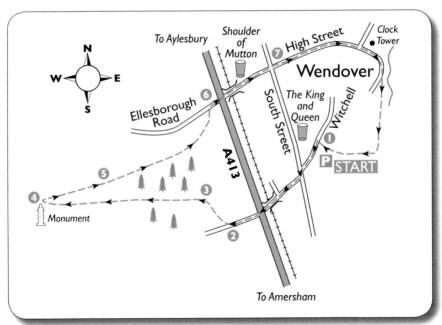

Welcome' kissing gate and continue ahead through the trees. After about a mile into the walk, you come to a metal gate on your right. Go through the gate, passing a National Trust '**Coombe Hill**' sign. Now walk out from the trees and straight on ahead, looking out for a wooden fingerpost pointing the way 'To the monument 5 mins'. Follow the gravel path past gorse and blackberries to the monument. Then stop to admire the wonderful views over the Vale of Aylesbury. *The monument was built in 1904 to commemorate the Boer War of 1899-1902. There is a helpful pillar in front of the monument which is a trig point with a plaque on it explaining the view. You can clearly see Chequers to the south and Waddesdon Manor in the opposite direction. There is also a small sign on the monument saying how it was struck by lightning and destroyed in 1938, but was rebuilt the same year by Buckinghamshire County Council.*

4 When you have finished at the monument, head back the way you came, but on a slightly lower, grassy path, keeping the gravel path up on your right. Pass a green post with an acorn on it, then a National Trust 'Coombe Hill' sign and go through a metal gate and back into the woods. Walk across the bridleway and follow the **Ridgeway** immediately opposite you, going through another metal gate.

5 You are now on my favourite part of the walk, with lovely open views of the Chilterns, and safe off-lead time for your dog. When you get to a sign on your right for Bacombe Hill, turn sharp left and follow the path downhill. Go through a kissing gate with an acorn national trail sign on it. The woods you walked through at the start are up on your right. The path gradually leads downhill and away from the woods. When you get to another green post, take the lower path, heading towards Wendover in the vale below. *The chalk that forms the Chiltern Hills is visible in the path as you walk. This area is a Site of Special Scientific Interest and is home to many rare wild flowers, such as orchids and the Chiltern gentian. In the summer you are surrounded by shimmering butterflies, with the hum of crickets in the grass and kites circling in the skies above.* Pass a bench and another sign for the Ridgeway and continue on this path. You eventually come to some wooden steps, with evidence of quarrying by the path. Walk to a metal gate, then down to **Ellesborough Road**.

6 Cross the road and turn right, walking over a road bridge (the bridge you crossed at the start is to your right) then into Wendover. Pass the Shoulder of Mutton and a chocolate-box row of cottages. Then you can either shorten the walk by turning right into South Street to your car, or continue the walk into **Wendover**.

7 Walk down the **High Street** passing a variety of pubs, cafés and independent shops. Just before the clock tower, turn right and follow the **Heron Path**. The old building you pass on your left behind the brick wall was once Wendover Junior School, now it's been converted into houses with roses growing over the wall. Follow the footpath by the side of Hampden Meadow, then the cricket field with the stream always on your left. By a Ridgeway sign and dog bin, turn right and walk up **Chapel Lane**, then through the gate to return to the car park.

Standing by the Monument on top of Coombe Hill.

The impressive Wendover Clock Tower is an early Victorian structure, built in 1842 as a market hall. It kept its basic form until 1870, when it was decided that this was the ideal place to park the village fire engine. At the same time a lock-up was created for the growing number of Wendover miscreants and the tower was extended to 58 ft to house the clock and bell. If you look closely, you can see the cut-away brickwork of the support piers put in to accommodate the fire engine. Today, the criminals and the fire engine have moved out while the Tourist Information Centre has moved in.

Tring Reservoirs and Towpaths

The perfect setting for a waterside walk.

These reservoirs were built in the 1800s to provide water for the Grand Union Canal. This is a truly waterside walk as you start and end on the Grand Union Canal, walk round four reservoirs in the middle, along a short stretch of the Wendover Arm then finish with a leisurely stroll by the Aylesbury Arm. Dogs who love water will be in heaven while birdwatchers don't have to dread your arrival as the Wilstone Reservoir has steep walls leaving water birds safe from curious dogs. There are a couple of farm fields where your dog will need to be on a lead, but other than that most of this walk is relaxed off-lead time far away from roads and livestock.

The Chilterns – A Dog Walker's Guide

Terrain
There are no gradients on this walk. The towpaths might be muddy in the middle of the winter, but the paths round the reservoirs are all well maintained making this easy walking in all weather. There are grass footpaths across two fields in the middle of the walk.

Where to park
There is plenty of parking at Startop's End pay and display car park where the walk starts. There are two prices, £1.50 for up to 3 hours or £3 for up to 24 hours. You should be able to do this walk within the 3 hour slot. For satnav, the postcode for the Anglers Retreat is HP23 4LJ.

How to get there
The car park is just north of Tring on the B489. If you are coming from the south, the car park is just before the traffic lights on the bridge over the canal.

Refreshments
The Anglers Retreat is almost opposite the car park. It has a beer garden, good quality home cooked food and is dog and child friendly ☎ 01442 822250. Half way round the walk you pass the Half Moon in Wilstone ☎ 01442 826410.

Dog factors
. . . .
Distance: 4¾ miles
Road walking: Through the village of Wilstone, and about 30 yards along a pavement to Tringford reservoir.
Livestock: Water birds by the reservoirs and sheep in the fields at point 4.
Stiles: None
Nearest vets: Watermead Surgery, 11 Lakeside, Watermead, Aylesbury HP19 0FX ☎ 01296 745373, or Springwell Veterinary Surgery, 98 Western Road, Tring, Hertfordshire HP23 4BJ ☎ 01442 822151

The Walk
. . . .

1 Follow the gravel path from the back of the car park. There are often fishermen along here and my whippet can't resist going to say hello and checking out their bait, but as long as you have recall your dog is safe off lead here. You follow the **Grand Union Canal** for about 50 yards before you take the right fork to walk by **Startop's End** reservoir. At the next junction, turn right again and follow a raised path between Startop's End and Marsworth reservoirs. There's a whole row of bins along here which is very handy for dog walkers at the start of a walk. When you cross a small footbridge put your dog back on the lead as there is a road ahead.

② Cross the road, then turn right and follow the footpath until you get to the northern tip of **Tringford** reservoir. Now turn left to follow the signed footpath round the reservoir. This is a lovely shady spot as you walk under trees, passing a bird hide on your right. It's also safe off-lead time again. Follow the path until you come to a gate that leads onto a track. Go through the gate, then turn right and follow the track in the same direction until it becomes a road.

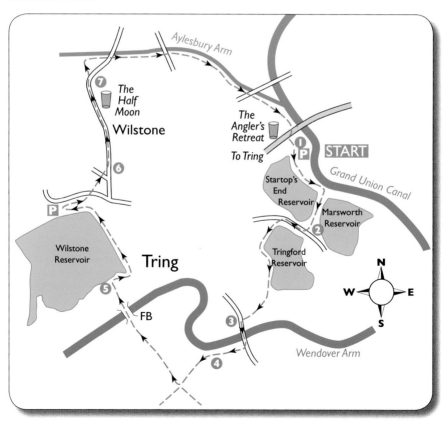

A dapper Welsh Terrier by the Aylesbury Arm.

3 When you come to the road, turn left and walk uphill past a row of cottages, then a few yards without a pavement as you cross a small bridge over the **Wendover Arm**. On the other side of the road, turn right down a path to the canal. Follow the Wendover Arm for a short stretch.

4 As the canal widens and curves to the right, follow the footpath ahead, leaving the canal behind. You come to a metal gate and cross path. Now your dog needs to go back on his lead as there are sheep ahead. Go through the gate, turn right and go through another metal gate to walk ahead along the right-hand side of two fields. This is where you will find the sheep but it's a large field so there is plenty of space between your hound and the sheep. A kissing gate on the other side takes you to a section of the Wendover Arm that is in the process of being restored. Cross the canal using the wooden footbridge and turn right on the other side. After a few yards, go through the metal swing gate on your left. Follow a tree-lined path gently downhill to a cross-track.

5 Turn right and walk for about 200 yards, then look out for a track on your left that takes you to the banks of the **Wilstone** reservoir. When you get to the other end of the reservoir, go down some steps to a car park. Turn right and walk through the car park, then keep walking following the hedge with the steep slope up to the reservoir on your right. After about 30 yards there is a footpath sign and a gap in the hedge. Cross the road with care and follow the path opposite, diagonally right across a field to a gate, followed by a small footbridge then a track. Cross the track and follow a grassy path over another footbridge to a lane.

6 You are now on the edge of **Wilstone**. Turn left and walk through the village, passing cottages, a war memorial, village store and pub. *This peaceful English village was the scene of mob riots and the murder of an elderly couple, John and Ruth Osbourn, in the mid 18th century. The couple were turned away from a farm after begging for food. When the farmer's cows became ill, he blamed the couple and accused Ruth of witchcraft. Trial by ducking was considered the best way to discover their guilt or innocence. The couple were taken into Tring workhouse to escape the growing mob who were hunting for them. But the crowd smashed their way into the workhouse. After threatening to burn the whole village down, the mob dragged the terrified couple to Wilstone pond where they were subsequently drowned. The government could not allow such civic disobedience. They made an example of a chimney sweep, Thomas Colley, who apparently had been one of the keenest in the ducking trial. He was hanged and his body was left in chains for years afterwards as a deterrent to others.*

7 At the top of this road you come to a children's playground and a recreation area, a popular spot with Wilstone dogs who like to chase a ball. Turn left at the corner of the play area and follow the path to the canal. Now turn right and follow the towpath by the side of the **Aylesbury Arm**. This peaceful stretch is perfect for off-lead time. The canal eventually joins the **Grand Union Canal** and you pass some boats on permanent moorings. When you come to a bridge with a white house on the right, go up the steps to the road. The car park is almost directly opposite you.

Aldbury and the Ashridge Estate

By the village pond in Aldbury.

It is well worth spending some time in this quintessential English village with its excellent pubs, duck pond on a green, thatched cottages and even stocks. What's more, it has its own Morris Men who perform in the summer months. The idyllic location has made this village popular with film makers, *The Dirty Dozen*, *The Avengers*, *Inspector Morse* and *Midsomer Murders* have all had scenes filmed here. The Ashridge Estate covers 5,000 acres of the Chiltern Hills and this walk takes you through beech and oak woodlands which are carpeted with bluebells in spring. There's plenty of space for dogs to explore and when you reach the monument you're sure to find some other dogs to meet and greet, as well as a café and visitor centre for the human walkers. The return journey takes you back through the woods to this lovely village.

Terrain

Uphill at the start then it levels off, and downhill on the way back. I would recommend wearing decent walking shoes for this walk.

Where to park

There is a small car park next to the village pond. (GR 965124) **OS map:** Explorer 181 Chiltern Hills North.

How to get there

Aldbury is a few miles east of Tring. From the A41, take the A4251, then turn left onto Newground Road. Head for the northern edge of the village and the green.

Refreshments

You will be spoilt for choice on this walk. The Greyhound Inn overlooks the duck pond ☎ 01442 851228, and you pass the Valiant Trooper at the start of the walk ☎ 01442 851203. Both pubs come highly recommended, serve food and have picnic tables outside. Brownlow café is in the middle of the walk by the monument and visitor centre. It remembers its four-legged customers with dog treats and a water bowl for thirsty hounds. There are also benches near the monument for picnickers.

Dog factors

Distance: 2½ miles
Road walking: You walk along the pavement in Aldbury at the start and end of the walk.
Livestock: There are fallow and muntjac deer on the Ashridge Estate. If you think your dog could chase them or wouldn't reliably come back if called, keep him on a lead to protect the deer, and your dog, if he runs after a deer into a road.
Stiles: None
Nearest vets: Barton Lodge Veterinary Centre, 1 Midland Road, Hemel Hempstead, Hertfordshire HP2 5BH ☎ 01442 216048

The Walk

1 From the village green, walk past the stocks and the shop. Turn right down **Trooper Road** and then left at the Valiant Trooper. Turn left again into **Newground Road**. After the road veers to the right turn left into **Malting**

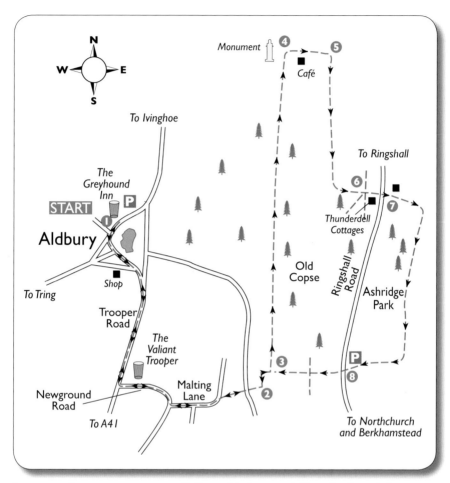

Lane passing pretty cottages. Follow this lane uphill and when it becomes a private drive on the left, turn half-left following the bridleway signed to Berkhamsted Common and the Chiltern Way (don't follow the footpath). Keep your dog close as you soon come to a road that you have to cross. Follow the path opposite, uphill through the trees for about 30 yards. Dogs are fine off-lead now.

2 You now come to a path crossing your route and a wooden signpost with arrows pointing off in various directions. Turn left for about 30 yards. Look out for a tree on your left with an arrow on it and the mark 'CW'. Turn right now and go up a steep bank – don't worry it's a short stretch and is the steepest part of the walk. Pass an open grassy area on your left then walk under electricity wires. After about 30 yards you come to a gravel track.

3 Turn left and follow this wide level path for about ½ mile, passing blackberry bushes and large beech trees with the occasional view across to Aldbury through the trees on your left. When you pass a sign for 'Old Copse Trail' the path begins to go uphill. Put your dog back on a lead now as there is a car park ahead. Pass the cars and you will find yourself at the edge of a large grassy area with the monument on your left, the café and toilets on your right and a few benches dotted round the edges. An excellent spot for a picnic!

The Ashridge Estate began as a monastery in the early 13th century. In Tudor times the buildings were extended and Henry VIII and his children were regular visitors. The park was designed by the famous landscape architect Capability Brown in the 1760s, and during the two World Wars the house was used to train and billet troops. The huge granite Bridgewater Monument was built in 1832 to honour the third Duke of Bridgewater's canal building successes and to celebrate the canal era. It is a Grade II listed monument with 172 steps that you can climb to admire the view over the Chilterns, although your dog would have to keep his four paws firmly on the ground.

4 When you are ready to move on, take the path in front of the café and walk with the café on your right and the monument behind you. Follow this wide surfaced path heading towards **Ashridge Park**. After about 50 yards look out for a metal barrier on your right, set a little way back from the main path.

5 Turn right here to walk past the barrier and head back into the woods. This wide path leads you through dappled shade and under mature beech trees. You could let your dog off the lead as there are no roads, but the woods are full of deer so keep him close by. When you come to a path running parallel with a meadow, turn left and follow the path with the meadow on your right and woods on the left. At the end of the meadow there is a footpath sign. Turn left here and follow the path through the trees. You pass open glades in the wood as you walk where the trees have been cut down. It is quite sociable as the woods are popular with local dog walkers. The path ends at a 5-way junction.

6 Take the second path on your left, heading east along a rutted grassy path. You pass rhododendron bushes on the left and soon you begin to see a meadow on your right. The path ends by the side of **Thunderdell Cottages** (they are marked on the OS map to help you navigate) and **Ringshall Road**.

7 Cross the road and walk straight ahead through the gates into Ashridge

Estate, passing the pretty **Thunderdell Lodge** on your left with its chequerboard brickwork. Follow the wide surfaced path ahead past large beech trees. When this path turns to the left, the walk turns right, to follow the signpost and the **Chiltern Way** footpath. Pass a yellow post and walk with the meadow on your left and the wood on the right. The path comes to a bridleway and fingerpost. Turn right here. Keep your dog close as you are about to come to a small parking area and a road.

8 Cross the road and follow the sign opposite through the woods, heading west. You will find yourself by **Woodsby Cottage**. Turn left and walk to the fingerpost sign then turn right on the bridleway. Continue

The splendid Bridgewater Monument is in the shape of a fluted Greek Doric column.

ahead past a fingerpost marked 'Chiltern Way bridleway' and continue in the same direction. You will soon recognize where you are, as you now retrace your steps back to **Aldbury**. Go down the steep slope and this time turn left. Turn right at the footpath sign and down a slope to the road. Cross the road and walk back to the village.

Berkhamsted, Castle Ruins and a Canal

The end of the walk follows the towpath by the Grand Union canal.

This walk follows a quiet country lane before crossing large arable fields and woods where your dog is free to run and explore. You then come to Berkhamsted, passing the ruins of the Norman castle, and three dog-friendly pubs all along a picturesque stretch of the Grand Union Canal with tables at the front where you can sit and watch the world pass by. Towpaths are ideal for dog walkers as you can relax without worrying about roads or sudden fields of sheep. My dog was very content and thoroughly worn out after this varied walk.

The Chilterns – A Dog Walker's Guide

Terrain
This would be a good winter walk as it is level and mainly along surfaced paths.

Where to park
There is a free small car park at the junction of Bullbeggars Lane and Bank Mill Lane (GR 006072). **OS Map:** Explorer 181 Chiltern Hills North.

How to get there
Heading east along the A4251, just on the eastern edge of Berkhamsted, turn up Bullbeggars Lane. Just over a small bridge there is a car park.

Refreshments
You walk past three pubs on the towpath, all with tables outside to sit and watch the world go by, and who all welcome dogs inside the bar area with water bowls and dog treats. And they also serve food for the tired owners. The Crystal Palace ☎ 01442 862998, the Boat ☎ 01442 877152 and the Rising Sun ☎ 01442 864913.

Dog factors
· ·

Distance: 5 miles
Road walking: There is about a mile along Bullbeggars Lane but this is very quiet. There are a few hundred yards along a busy road in Berkhamsted, then a short section along pavements to get to the towpath.
Livestock: None
Stiles: None
Nearest vets: St John's Veterinary Surgery, 320A High Street, Berkhamsted HP4 1HT ☎ 01442 863101

The Walk
· ·

1 Head up **Bullbeggars Lane**, first crossing a small bridge over the Grand Union Canal. You will be returning along this towpath at the end of the walk. The lane then crosses the railway track. Now follow this lane for about a mile. There might be the occasional car, but it's so quiet that you can hear anything coming from a long way off so there's plenty of time to get hold of your dog, and there are grassy verges on either side. There's an uphill stretch towards the end. As you see a wood ahead and a large house on the right, turn left on a footpath to enter the top of a large arable field.

2 Walk to the end of the field then continue ahead and downhill through woodland. Dogs can be off lead here and it is total dog heaven! Come out of the wood to follow a narrow path that is fenced on either side, so your dog can stay off lead. Keep going in the same direction until the track becomes a lane with houses on your left. It would be as well to put your pooch back on a lead now in case he decides to explore the gardens. The lane ends with two large houses with dark wooden cladding. Cross the road and follow the bridleway opposite with trees on your right and more large houses on the left. Cross the next road and follow the bridleway opposite through a strip of woodland. After a few yards turn right at the track and you emerge from the woods by **Britwell Drive** and the manicured lawns of Castle Village.

3 You now need to follow the main road for a few hundred yards up to the Inns of Court war memorial and car park, passing **Berkhamsted Golf Club**.

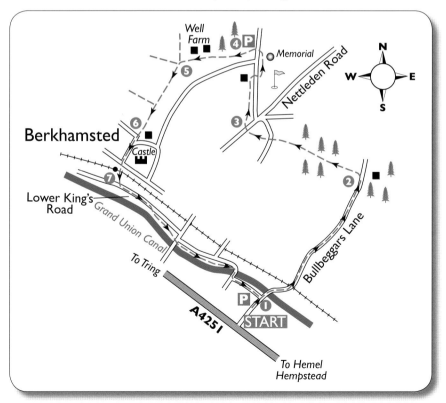

The Chilterns – A Dog Walker's Guide

When you get to the clubhouse on your left, it might be easier to cross the road and skirt along the edge of the golf course to the war memorial. Keep your dog under close control and wait if you see a golfer about to take a shot. At the war memorial, cross the road and head to the bridleway path in the far left corner of the car park.

There was a network of nearly eight miles of trenches dug near here during the First World War and you could make a small detour at this point to explore what remains (GR 998102). They were dug by the Inns of Court Officer Training Corps who were stationed in Berkhamsted during the war. The trenches were dug as a rehearsal for the battlefields of northern France and as general fitness training. There is an interpretation board by the trenches outlining the history of the troops billeted in Berkhamsted.

4 Walk down the bridleway along a pleasant path through woodland, there is a road on your left and **Well Farm** is ahead so it might be wise to keep your dog on a lead. Ignore any cross tracks and pass another path leading to the trenches. The route leads to a farm track and past paddocks and stables. After the stables, look out for a metal kissing gate on your left.

5 Go through the gate and now enjoy walking along the bottom of the valley with sweeping views across the landscape. Cross three meadows, then walk by a cricket pitch and tennis courts. The last part of this footpath passes by a school so make sure your dog is safely back on the lead for the last section.

6 Turn left and follow the pavement down **Castle Hill** then ahead under the railway bridge after stopping to admire the castle ruins on your left. *The castle dates from the 11th to 13th centuries. Originally a motte and bailey castle was built on the site by Robert Mortain, half-brother of William the Conqueror. The castle was rebuilt by Thomas Becket in the 12th century. It has been home to Plantagenet princes and the Black Prince and is now managed by English Heritage. It is free to visit, open every day and dogs on leads are welcome.*

7 Under the railway bridge turn left on **Lower Kings Road** to follow the towpath by the side of the **Grand Union Canal**. There is a large totem pole on the opposite bank, carved from Canadian red cedar wood. It was gifted to a local businessman in the 1960s and looks rather out of place in Berkhamsted! Follow the path past three pubs, all with outside seating areas, until you come to bridge number 143, where you cross the canal to continue along the opposite bank. At bridge number 144, leave the towpath and walk up to the road, then turn right to return to the parking area.

To the Top of Ivinghoe Beacon

Following the Ridgeway to the top of Ivinghoe Beacon.

Ivinghoe Beacon crowns the Chilterns escarpment and is the point where the Ridgeway starts and ends. There are also the remains of an Iron Age hill fort on the beacon summit. The Ridgeway was favoured by drovers taking their animals to market over the centuries due to the good visibility and firm ground. Modern walkers appreciate this high path for the same qualities and it is always a popular route with dog walkers. The circuit is easy to navigate as you can see the chalk path snaking ahead of you over the undulating landscape. You get a great sense of satisfaction standing at the top of Ivinghoe Beacon with the wind in your hair and an amazing view across the Vale of Aylesbury and Dunstable Downs. If you are worried about the gradient, I met a Chihuahua on the summit – if his little legs can get to the top, then this route should be no problem for the larger breeds – or their owners!

The Chilterns – A Dog Walker's Guide

Terrain
These chalk hills are covered with springy grassland and hawthorn scrub. The walk mainly follows high ground, so although it might be windy in the winter, you are less likely to get bogged down in the mud. Although some of the walk is level, there are also up and downhill sections with a short steep ascent to the summit of Ivinghoe Beacon.

Where to park
Ivinghoe Beacon National Trust car park has plenty of space and is a popular spot for people flying model gliders (GR 964159). **OS Map:** Explorer 181 Chiltern Hills North.

How to get there
Ivinghoe Beacon lies 5 miles north-east of Tring. The car park is signed on a small road heading south from the B489.

Refreshments
There is often an ice cream van in the National Trust car park. The family-friendly Rose and Crown is just over a mile away in the village of Ivinghoe and welcomes dogs on a lead in the bar and garden. This free house serves food every day except Sunday evenings and Mondays. It is a popular spot with walkers and they advise booking a table at the weekends. ☎ 07585 776987 Postcode LU7 9EQ.

Dog factors

Distance: 3½ miles
Road walking: None, although you have to cross two roads.
Livestock: Keep an eye out for sheep before letting your dog off the lead. There may be sheep in a field at point 5.
Stiles: None
Nearest vets: Watermead Surgery, 11 Lakeside, Watermead, Aylesbury HP19 0FX ☎ 01296 745373, or Springwell Veterinary Surgery, 98 Western Road, Tring, Hertfordshire HP23 4BJ ☎ 01442 822151

The Walk

1 From the middle of the car park, carefully cross the road and walk up the path opposite, passing hawthorn bushes and scrub. You shortly come to a cross track where you turn left and walk with the road close by on your left. The path ends with a car park on your left. Turn right here and follow the path to a gate into the **Ashridge Estate**.

2 Through the gate you find yourself on top of a large hill. Turn right and follow the top of the hill on the **Ridgeway** heading north. The walk starts to head steeply down with a view across the valley to Ivinghoe on your left, and the Ivinghoe Hills ahead. You can clearly see the path ahead as the grass has been worn down by walkers to reveal the chalk the hills are formed from. When you pass a sign for Ashridge Estate Boundary Trail, put your dog on a lead as **Beacon Road** is ahead.

3 Cross the road and follow the path directly ahead along short springy turf to the top of **Ivinghoe Beacon** and that amazing view. *As you walk, look to your*

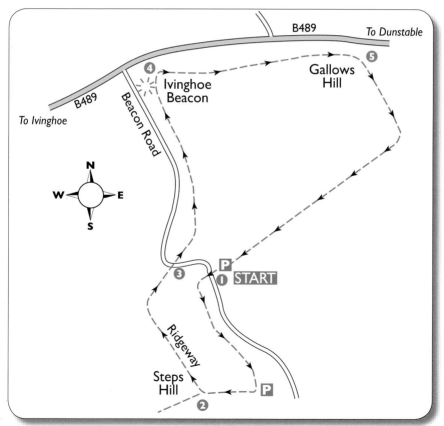

The Chilterns – A Dog Walker's Guide

Chalk downland on the Ivinghoe Hills.

right for a view of the Whipsnade Chalk Lion on the Dunstable Downs. It was built in the 1930s as an advertisement for the zoo. It is so prominent that during the Second World War it was covered with netting, turf and paint to stop the Luftwaffe using it for navigation. The lion is home to a colony of cavies and wallabies who have strayed out of the zoo and settled on the Downs.

4 Turn right from the top of the Beacon and follow the undulating path along the ridge towards **Gallows Hill**. Go through a gate and continue ahead until you come to a second gate with the lion now ahead of you.

5 Turn right and walk down the side of a field with a fence on your left. There may be sheep in this field. Go through a gate at the bottom of the field then walk ahead between two large fields. Turn right at the corner and walk towards the car park which is on top of the hill ahead of you. Go through another gate, then uphill to return to the car park. When you get to the top, turn back and admire the view as you can see half the walk spread out before you.

Dunstable Downs and Whipsnade Tree Cathedral

Posing poodles on Dunstable Downs.

The **Chilterns Gateway Centre is perched on top** of the Dunstable Downs and is an excellent spot to start this walk from. It is very dog-friendly with free dog bags and water bowls. There is plenty of seating outside with a panoramic view across the Dunstable Downs and Ivinghoe Hills. You could bring a kite or buy one in the shop as this is the most amazing place to fly one. Otherwise, sit back and watch as the skies are filled with the flutter of kites.

The Downs are popular with Dunstable dog walkers, so it's a sociable walk for dogs and owners, with stunning views and an interesting Tree Cathedral to explore half way round. Trees and shrubs were planted in the shape of a medieval cathedral after the First World War in the spirit of 'faith, hope and reconciliation'. In summer, the open glades of chalk grassland are carpeted with wild flowers making this high spot a wonderful place to be.

The Chilterns – A Dog Walker's Guide

Dog factors

Distance: 2½ miles
Road walking: There is a short section along a surfaced lane.
Livestock: Goats in a field as we were walking back from the Tree Cathedral.
Stiles: None
Nearest vets: Noah's Ark Veterinary Clinic, 54 High Street South, Dunstable LU6 3HD ☎ 01582 606466

Terrain
Chalk grasslands and surfaced paths make this route easy walking.

Where to park
The National Trust pay and display car park at the Chilterns Gateway Centre. (GR 008195) Postcode LU6 2GY

How to get there
The Chilterns Gateway Centre is on the B4541 south-west of Dunstable. It is clearly signed.

Refreshments
There is a National Trust café in the visitor centre with plenty of picnic tables outside. The café also has dog bowls and provides free dog bags.

The Walk

1 From the car park, head for the 'Pedestrian Exit', then follow the gravel path away from the visitor centre and aim for the woods ahead of you. Walk under power cables to the edge of the wood where you will see a footpath sign. It says left to Whipsnade Tree Cathedral and right to Whipsnade Downs. Turn left and follow the bridleway along a shady path beside the trees.

2 After about 200 yards you come to a footpath post. Here the path forks and you take the path on your right into pretty mixed woodland. Pass **Ever Green Lodge** on your left and then follow a surfaced path. Pass Swallowsprings and continue ahead, be aware that there is the occasional car on this wide surfaced lane. Pass a sign for **Swallow Springs Nature Reserve** on your left and as you walk, look out for a 'National Trust Whipsnade' sign on your right.

3 At this point leave the track and follow the path. Pass the Whipsnade Jubilee Orchard on your left and go through a swing gate into **Whipsnade Tree Cathedral**. Take some time to explore this amazing place. Then head for the information board, you will see a small car park through a gate on your left. Walk past the board to a narrow grassy footpath. This is the **Icknield Way**. Turn right and follow the path with the cathedral on your right. Go through a metal kissing gate and follow the signs for 'Whipsnade Circular Walk'. The path now follows the side of a large field with a metal kissing gate on the

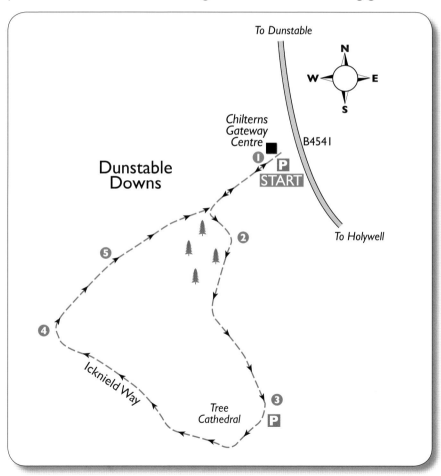

other side. There were goats in the corner of this field the last time I passed. Continue ahead a few yards to a footpath sign.

4 Turn right and walk ahead down a shady tunnel with plenty of interesting smells for dogs who can safely be off lead here. There is a slight gradient but it is very gradual and you emerge from this path to a stunning view towards the Ivinghoe Hills. Follow the path for about 20 yards to a metal gate on your right and a sign for the Chiltern Gateway Centre.

5 Now follow a grassy path by the side of a field with wild flowers and the hum of insects in summer. Down on your left you can watch the gliders taking off and landing at London Gliding Club and there is a bench positioned for the perfect view. Soon you will spot the kites in the sky as you approach the **Chilterns Gateway Centre**. Go through a metal gate and turn immediately right to walk up some wooden steps and cross the field back to the car park.

Exploring Whipsnade Tree Cathedral.

Walking above Totternhoe

Chalk loving wildflowers grow by the path.

This walk takes you into another world as you follow the path from Totternhoe up to a medieval quarry that has long since returned to nature. The slopes are now covered with wild flowers, cowslips and orchids. In summer look out for butterflies on the flower-filled slopes. There is a population of the rare Duke of Burgundy butterfly, as well as chalk hill blues and the small blue. This high ground also provides commanding views across the Dunstable Downs, Ivinghoe Beacon and the chalk lion at Whipsnade zoo. We met some very friendly dog walkers here, and there is plenty of space for dogs to run around and explore. Totternhoe clunch has been quarried from this site for centuries. You can see the chalk in the paths as you walk. Its chalk has been used in Westminster Abbey and Windsor Castle.

The Chilterns – A Dog Walker's Guide

Terrain

If you start from the Cross Keys there is a short steep stretch at the start, then it is easy level walking along grassy paths. You can avoid this uphill section by starting from the NT car park.

Where to park

You can park at the Cross Keys if you are eating there. The directions for this walk start from the pub (GR 980218). Alternatively park in the National Trust car park which is off Castle Hill Road between Castle Close and Park Avenue (GR 986217). From the far side of the car park, walk up the steps and turn right then follow the path towards point 2 of the route. **OS map:** Explorer 193 Luton and Stevenage.

How to get there

Totternhoe is 2 miles west of Dunstable. From the B489 heading west, turn right on the roundabout towards Totternhoe. One mile from the roundabout, turn right up a signed track to the National Trust car park and picnic site, or continue through Totternhoe to the Cross Keys pub.

Refreshments

The 17th-century Cross Keys pub is Grade II listed and is a lovely spot to sit and relax before or after the walk. Dogs are welcome in the beer garden, which has an impressive view across the Downs, and in the bar area. It serves food every day. ☎ 01525 220434 Postcode LU6 2DA

Dog factors

Distance: 3 miles
Road walking: None
Livestock: None
Stiles: None
Nearest vets: Noah's Ark Veterinary Clinic, 54 High Street South, Dunstable LU6 3HD ☎ 01582 606466

The Walk

1 Take the public footpath opposite the Cross Keys pub. This steep path quickly takes you away from the sound of the traffic below and is safe for your dog to be off lead. At the top you meet a path where you turn right along a level path, and you are rewarded for your climb with some good views to the right.

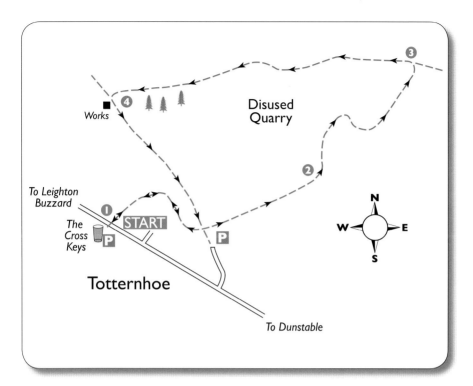

When you come to a fork in the path take the left option. There is another uphill section now but with fences and arable fields on either side of the path. Your dog can trot along at his own pace while you can have the odd rest to admire the panoramic views and catch your breath.

❷ Follow the edge of the quarry and at the far side turn left to follow the grass path along the other edge of the quarry then downhill on a wide grassy path, now with the quarry on your left and the view ahead.

❸ You come to a track where you can clearly see the white chalk this hill is formed from. Here you turn left to follow the **Icknield Way** downhill, passing an interesting wooden painted wild flower mural. There may be horses in the field on the left, but they are fenced off from the path. Continue ahead in the same direction until you come to a T-junction in front of **Totternhoe Lime and Stone Company** and a footpath sign.

❹ Here you turn left. Follow the footpath until you come to a T-junction. A quick left then right turn takes you down the steps to the NT car park.

Meeting two Yorkshire Terriers on the Icknield Way.

Or turn right and retrace your steps to the left turn and walk downhill to the road opposite the **Cross Keys** pub.